WHAT IS DRIVING
WOMEN TO DRUG USE
AND HOW YOU CAN HELP
Psychology and Behavioral Sciences of Addiction

DR. RICHARD CORKER-CAULKER, PHD, EDDCP

WESTBOW
PRESS
A DIVISION OF THOMAS NELSON

WestBow Press books may be ordered through booksellers or by contacting:

WestBow Press
A Division of Thomas Nelson
1663 Liberty Drive
Bloomington, IN 47403
www.westbowpress.com
1-(866) 928-1240

ISBN: 978-1-4497-8696-0 (sc)
ISBN: 978-1-4497-8698-4 (hc)
ISBN: 978-1-4497-8697-7 (e)

Library of Congress Control Number: 2013905257

Printed in the United States of America.

WestBow Press rev. date: 4/22/2013

DEDICATION

This book is dedicated to all descendants of the Kurkar/ Corker-Caulker family. Not forgetting, therapists and counselors serving individuals and families affected by the disease of addiction including all individual's battling with the disease of addiction.

ABSTRACT

Women relapse every day in America from different walks of life and social class or family groups. It is unfortunate that some even die in the process. From this study we found that majority of women use street drugs and alcohol because of social reason like being in the company of family members, friends or spouse who use, taking social professions with major problems and challenges, when relationship is not working right etc. Also, with the analysis tool use in the study clinicians can now analyze women triggers experience to determine categories, patterns and scale of risk for relapse prevention skill training. This is why this study is very important to be in the public domain to improve practice. We can now scientifically based drug and alcohol treatment planning on pre-treatment relapse trigger analysis. The fact is clear women diagnosed with addiction experienced various stimuli that become cues and triggered craving and addiction relapse through association with behavior leading to a reward (a drug high) or to relief of a negative state resulting from abstinence. When women with addiction disease undergo treatment and return to an environment in which they are subjected to the same triggers initially associated with their addictive behavior and relapsed, they experienced some difficulty staying clean and sober.

The purpose of this study was to collect data on individual trigger experiences to analyze and develop treatment support for women at risk of relapse. Eighteen women (ages 17–45) with a history of drug or alcohol addiction living in a treatment facility in the Inland Empire region of Southern California responded to a questionnaire containing both quantitative (Likert rating scale) and qualitative (open-ended questions) items regarding trigger experiences. Quantitative data were analyzed with descriptive statistics. Qualitative data were categorized according to content. Participants perceived relapse triggers to be related to family and financial problems, the desire to feel good, and relationship issues. Peer pressure was the most frequently cited reason for first using drugs or alcohol. Triggers for relapse and perceived risk factors also related most frequently to social and relationship issues and financial problems.

The researcher theorized drug use behavior of women is not related only to using to feel good or alters thoughts but social problems. Drug use occurred among women in a relationship context peer or group unit and that context, problems, stress and challenges in the context or relationship is what is driving women behavior because it constitutes and is consistent with the natural makeup and disposition of women. Women were created to respond to the solitary, lonesome and task assigned oriented environment created. A woman was created to complement and working alongside a spouse, family or a person to fulfill equally and collectively a responsibility giving and shared by both. Women's drug use behavior is driven not because of the drug but the personality, task, problems and challenges sometime unnecessary triggers present in the relationship and helping environment. Women use because they are in a relationship or unit of relationship (peer or group or person or friends) that uses and influences the drug use behavior. The researcher recognized exceptions. But the researcher also believed this is not blame game, shifting responsibility or making a person not to accept responsibility for their behavior, action and choices. Generally speaking, the same is true of girls who got pregnant before their college years or during their college years. They got pregnant not because they wanted to have sex or be pregnant but because they are in a complementing working relationship that made them pregnant. The general psychological research in the past for understanding human behavior states a person's behavior is driven by physical needs or instinct. This study shows otherwise. The researcher shows women's drug use behaviors are influenced not simply by instinct or a desire to satisfy physical needs, but by relationship, relationship problems, or unit of relationship peer or group or friends that do such things in concert. There are more social factors at play in women's prescription or street drug use. The researcher having worked the streets in the Inland Empire visiting individuals and their families diagnosed with addiction diseases has first hand experience in this matter. Women are driven and motivated by relationship rather than by physical needs, physical drive, or personality problems. This discovery in women's addiction behavior calls for a new approach how clinicians from now on continue assessment and planning interventions to minimize relapsing behaviors among women in and out of drug and alcohol treatment. Therefore, planning drug and alcohol treatment with goals and objectives only focus on thoughts, feelings and behavior will no longer be effective from the revelation discovered in this study. The social environment and all therein must be considered as comprehensive priority along side other variables.

Also, the author shows the main contributing factor for drug use among first-time women drug users is peer pressure and for ongoing users are relationship problems or group influence. Both unit peer and group are consistent with the makeup of women created to respond to the void cause by loneliness, lonesomeness, and the solitary lifestyle of their opposite sex. Therefore, the therapist planning intervention should find a way to include the addict in social challenges and key associations in therapy, or if this is not possible for lack of consent or time and cost, teach avoidance skills to prevent relapse.

Conjectures or general ideas about drug-use triggers are just not adequate to determine women's relapse triggers. Therefore, the use of assessment techniques like the one done in this study (qualitative assessment and analysis), is highly appropriate if one is trained in the knowledge and skills of conducting individual or group qualitative assessment and analysis. This is the new direction for treating women in the twenty-first century with addiction problems or recidivism.

Therapists or clinicians must find out about social struggles or challenges affecting the lives of an addict seeking treatment.

The good thing is that the researcher has provided contributing factors or insights on women's drug and alcohol triggers, symptoms, craving patterns, and factors providing positive and negative reinforcement of behaviors leading to relapse. Future treatment should focus on helping individual clients to identify influences on their behavior in order to build specific relapse prevention skills. The use of this qualitative instrument to identify addicts' socio-environmental relationships will help focus treatment on specific social triggers that are primarily the trigger for drug use behavior. It will bring down cost and prevent repeated relapse due to undiagnosed social-environmental triggers leading to drug use behavior and repeated relapse. It will help therapist and clinician decide quickly where to start treatment targeting drug use and behavior, symptom reduction, or addressing the pretreatment socio-environmental triggers and the drug behavior and relapse.

The fact is clients who did not get their socio-environmental pretreatment triggers addressed continue to relapse in spite of efforts to reduce relapse behavior. The reason is socio-environmental triggers were not primarily a focus of treatment, remain unresolved, and continue to hunt addicts and make it extremely difficult to focus on staying clean and sober. The use of the qualitative instrument as precursor completed in this study is the future of drug treatment and intervention.

Clinicians will continue to ask if they should focus on the socio-environmental triggers leading to drug use or just focus on drug use and minimize the behavior. The study shows both are essential and both will determine the future of drug and alcohol treatment. But therapists will have to be trained how to conduct qualitative analysis using the approach outlined in this study. One thing is clear in drug and alcohol treatment for women in the twenty-first century: the first cause of action is to assess the social triggers contributing to the relapse behavior and chemical dependence and impact. The major issue now is how this information will inform not drive treatment planning for women diagnosed with the disease of addiction.

TABLE OF CONTENTS

LIST OF TABLES

[LIST OF FIGURES]

[ACKNOWLEDGMENTS]

The author would like to express sincere gratitude to Dr. Akin Merino, Dr. Chia-Wen Hsieh, and Dr. James Smith for their invaluable support and guidance, and all participants in the study for embracing the research idea and for their time spent on the questionnaire. Without their contributions of time and resources, this study would not have been possible.

[CHAPTER ONE]

The Problem

The specific problem addressed by this study is the difficulty women who have undergone addiction treatment have maintaining abstinence when they return to an environment where they are subjected to the same cues that triggered their addictive behavior. Recovery programs need to target responses to those specific triggers and stressors that influence an individual's addictive behavior (Kelly, Gaither, and King, 2007). In order to change responses, it is important to know which specific stimuli are triggers of addictive behavior in a given individual. The present researcher addressed this question by studying in depth a number of women being treated for addictive disorders who were living in a shelter facility in the Inland Empire community.

PROBLEM BACKGROUND

Relapse after Treatment for Addiction Disorders

For individuals with substance use problems, various stimuli become cues that trigger craving and addiction relapse through association with behavior leading to a reward (for example, a drug high) (Kelly, et al., 2007). Research specifically investigating stimuli that trigger addictive behavior before an individual starts treatment may provide important information to help therapists improve treatment of substance use disorders. In particular, such research may increase the effectiveness of treatment programs in the Inland Empire region of California for women with drug or alcohol addiction disorders.

According to Young, Joe, Hassin, and St. Clair (2001), the rate of recidivism in the general population treated for substance use disorders is 86% within two years after treatment, with the majority of relapses occurring within six months. In order to help clients develop the skills needed to prevent a relapse when exposed to pre-treatment relapse triggers, therapists and counselors should not only learn about pretreatment addiction triggers but also learn how to identify such triggers in their clients.

This study aims to provide information on addiction relapse triggers to therapists or clinicians who facilitate alcohol and drug treatment and discharge preparedness. The focus is on providing this information to therapists and clinicians who cannot observe the pre-treatment addiction phase and lifestyle of their clients before those clients come for help or treatment (Patton, 2002). Information from the outcome of the study should broaden clinical understanding of pre-treatment triggers experienced daily by women with addictions and the ways in which these triggers affect their thoughts, feelings, and behavior.

Failure to understand and effectively respond to addiction triggers likely leads to future relapse if the client is discharged into the same community in which the pretreatment addictive behavior occurred (Kelly, et al., 2007). Systematic information describing pretreatment triggers experienced by women undergoing treatment for substance use disorders in Inland Empire facilities should be useful both in planning relapse intervention during group treatment and in subsequent prevention of early relapse.

Addiction Triggers

In the Inland Empire region of California, the challenges presented by ubiquitous addiction triggers are real and ongoing, both for women receiving treatment while living in the community and for those returning to the community after treatment. Women with addiction disorders that impacted or affected their lives in the community before they were arrested and who were referred for treatment may continue to have the compulsion to obtain and re-experience the effect of drugs if they are discharged into the same community. Thus, it is essential for any relapse prevention treatment method to respond to the individual triggers and stressors in the community (Kelly, et al., 2007).

The human brain creates a relationship between addictive behavior and addiction relapse triggers through its ability to learn to anticipate reactions to stimuli (Pate, 2009), as in Pavlov's classical conditioning paradigm (Carroll, 1998). Thus, after repeated pairing of a neutral stimulus with an unconditioned stimulus, the neutral stimulus becomes a cue that elicits the same response as the response to the original unconditioned stimulus. For example, a certain kind of music or a specific location associated with the experience of getting high after taking a drug can produce overwhelming memories or emotions leading to drug-seeking behavior (Jaffe, 2010).

A relapse trigger can be any person, place, thing, or situation that reminds a person of drug or alcohol use or other addictive behavior (Urell, 2010). Common triggers include being around people with whom one previously used drugs, having money, getting paid, drinking, being involved in a social situation, and experiencing certain affective states such as anxiety, depression, or joy (Carroll, 1998).

Scientific studies of the brain show us the physiological foundation for understanding triggers and how they can result in relapse. The part of the brain affected by environmental triggers has been identified as the amygdala (see Figure 1). The amygdala is a small, almond-shaped structure located in the temporal lobes of the brain near the hippocampus. It is believed to be linked to individual emotions, behavior, and aggression, and it controls fear responses, secretion of hormones, arousal, and the formulation of emotional memories (Cherry, n.d.). The lateral section of the amygdala receives input from the visual, auditory, somato sensory, and pain systems. The medial nucleus of the amygdala is connected to the olfactory system. The central nucleus connects with brainstem areas that control the expression of innate behavior associated with physiological responses (Le Doux, 2008).

Most of the input to the amygdala involves excitatory pathways that use glutamate as a transmitter system. Thus, epinephrine, dopamine, serotonin, and acetylcholine are released in the amygdala, which is responsible for influencing the ways that excitatory and inhibitory neurons interact (Le Doux, 2008). Le Doux found that the neural input from an unconditioned stimulus and that of a conditioned stimulus both go to the same cells, and this convergence results in molecular responses that lead to synthesis of proteins that help strengthen and stabilize the conditioned response. Thus, through association with the drug experience, various environmental, social, or emotional stimuli can become cues that trigger the same physiological processes as the drug.

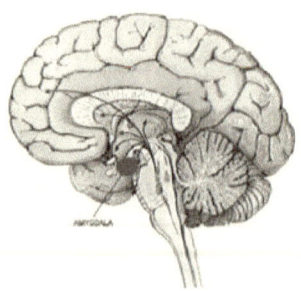

Figure 1.
The human brain and position of the amygdala. Source: Mathison, Alexander, and Rizzo (n.d.).

Research sponsored by the National Institute of Drug Abuse further investigated the role of the amygdala and adjoining structures in the effects of drug use (Koob and Le Moal, 2008). The researchers found that dopamine, a chemical messenger associated with pleasure and movement, plays a role, for example, in accounting for the addictive effects of cocaine. If the dopamine component in areas of the extended amygdala in rats is activated by a trigger, the high levels of dopamine resulting from overstimulation will cause the number of dopamine receptors (i.e., the molecules to which the dopamine binds) to increase, thereby causing the cocaine "high." After rats were trained to self-administer cocaine, the researchers inactivated dopamine components in areas of the extended amygdala in those rats. As a result, the rats not only significantly reduced the amount of cocaine they gave themselves but also increased dopamine overstimulation.

An individual's environment, thoughts, physical sensations, or behaviors that are repeatedly associated with the drug experience will likely become triggers for relapse.

Difficulty of Preventing Relapse

Addiction has been defined as a chronic relapsing disorder. As such, it is characterized by the following components: compulsion to seek and take the drug, loss of self-limiting control, and a negative emotional state resulting from abstinence (Koob and Le Moal, 2008). Koob and Le Moal's (2008) antireward system of the action of addiction on the brain can be used to explain the power of addiction, even after long-term abstinence. These authors expressed the process of addiction in terms of the reactive brain. During the process, the natural motivational system of rewards within the brain is transformed from a system of positive reinforcement to one of negative reinforcement (antireward), which acts to limit the rewards triggered by excessive reward system activity (for example, resulting from continuous drug exposure), providing a powerful motivation for the drug-seeking and drug-taking behavior that is associated with compulsive use (figure 2).

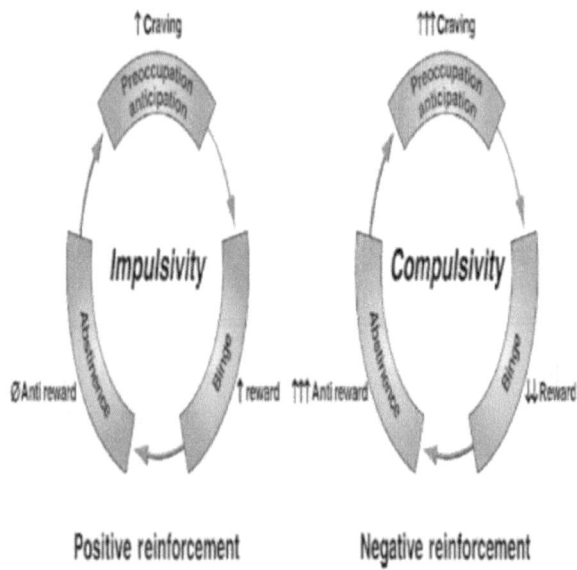

Figure 2.

Illustration of the movement from impulsivity to compulsivity and the shift from positive reinforcement associated with a binge component to negative reinforcement associated with withdrawal (taken from Koob and Le Moal, 2008, p. 54).

As hypothesized by Koob and Le Moal, craving increases compulsivity because of increased need for the drug resulting both from the loss of the positive reinforcement effect of the drug and from the creation of an antireward state supporting negative reinforcement (Koob and Le Moal, 2008, p. 54).

This dysregulation of the motivational systems persists even during long-term abstinence, creating a vulnerability to relapse triggers and craving (Koob and Le Moal, 2008). Some researchers have suggested that craving and the renewal of drug-seeking behavior after abstinence is induced by various triggers, such as direct reexposure to the drug, specific cues that the individual associates with taking the drug (external/internal triggers), and other experiences of stress (internal triggers) (Stewart, 2008).

Drug addiction creates long-lasting, cumulative changes in the brain that promote a vulnerability to relapse from either internal or external triggers (Porrino, et al., 2004; Stewart, 2008). Internal and external triggers are paired with the effects of the drug within the brain and thus remain capable of eliciting drug-seeking behavior (craving), even after a long period of abstinence (Stewart, 2008).

Although research has demonstrated some success in reducing relapse behaviors, because the complexity of craving triggers creates different experiences for every individual (Addolorato, Leggio, Abenavoli, and Gasbarrini, 2005), it is important to identify the *specific* triggers that cause an individual to experience craving, and the various symptoms associated with craving, relapse behaviors, and addiction pathways, so that appropriate responses can be developed to avoid relapse.

PURPOSE OF THE STUDY

The purpose of the current study was to assess pre-treatment relapsed trigger experiences of women with addictive disorders and ascertain why women are using drugs and alcohol. The objective was to collect data that would be representative of trigger experiences and that could then be analyzed to enhance understanding and to develop treatment support for women who experience a relapse caused by triggers.

Psychosocial treatments for addiction maintain a focus on abstinence as well as the development of both social and coping skills in order to produce individual success in terms of non-addictive behavior and a healthy, productive life (Beck, 1993; Kelly, et al., 2007; Miller and Rollnick, 2009). The particular triggers and stressors precipitating an individual's addictive behavior require identification so that treatment can be individualized to successfully prevent or minimize relapse (Kelly, et al., 2007).

Several methods have been proposed as a means of guiding the individual substance abuser through the process of identifying and understanding relapse triggers. These methods include cognitive-behavioral therapy, motivational interviewing, and acceptance-based coping intervention (Kelly, et al., 2007; Vieten, Astin, Buscemi, and

Galloway, 2010). The goals of these treatment programs focus on behavioral change (figure 3).

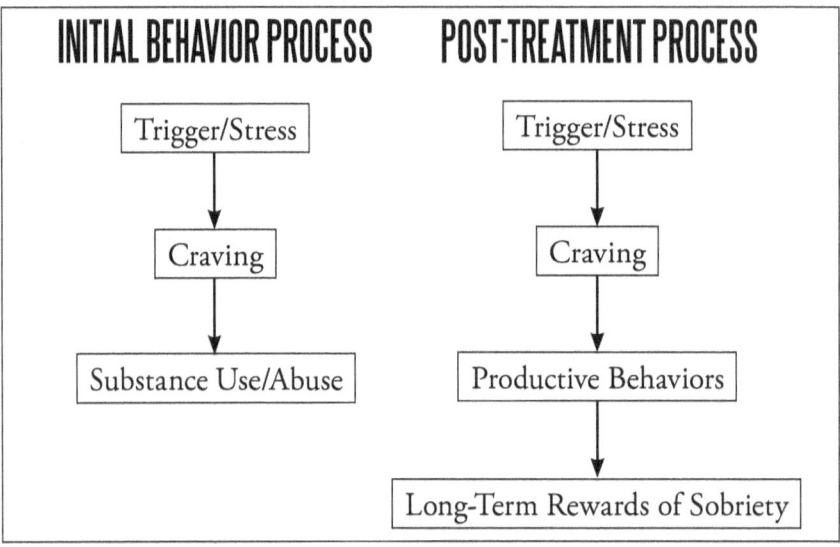

Figure 3.
Cognitive-behavioral therapy goal outline (adapted from Kelly, et al., 2007).

RESEARCH QUESTIONS

The following research questions were developed to guide the study:

1. How do women with addiction disorders who live in the Inland Empire region experience triggers of addiction relapse?
2. What are the contributing factors, patterns, and categories of addiction relapse triggers experienced by these women?
3. Are relapse triggers the same as the triggers of an individual's initial drug use?
4. What is perceived to be the most effective way for individuals in the Inland Empire community to respond to addiction relapse triggers?

LIMITATIONS AND DELIMITATIONS

The instrument used in gathering data for this analysis was a questionnaire which included a rating scale. Although effective in conducting research, such questionnaires may inadvertently leave out details or expression of feeling because the respondents are asked to rate their answers and also describe specific issues in their responses. It is also possible that the wording of the questions on the survey instrument may be misunderstood, thus reducing the comparability of responses. Furthermore, standardized questions do not allow respondents to express their thoughts naturally, because question and response categories are determined in advance, with responses rated and fixed. The respondents in this study were asked to fit their responses into what the questions were designed to find, rather than what they wanted to discuss. Furthermore, the data gathered in this study reflect the experiences of one specific group from a specific community, and it is not clear how far the conclusions of the study can be generalized. The researcher used a mixed research method for the study. The use of a mixed method may have brought bias to the results, specifically when analyzing the qualitative data.

SIGNIFICANCE OF THE STUDY

Contributions to the knowledge of relapse triggers among women with addiction in the Inland Empire region can serve as a basis for treatment and planning intervention to prevent relapse, and to improve program focus. Therefore, any organized information on addiction triggers resulting from the analysis of the data may serve to inform and enhance clinical practice. Triggers and stressors that lead to addiction relapse are generally specific (Kelly, et al., 2007). The study provides an opportunity to obtain data from a social context in which women with addiction disorders rate their individual experiences and describe the cues that trigger their addictive behavior.

The study used questions developed specifically to assess trigger experiences among clients of addiction programs in the Inland Empire region. The questions are not merely of academic interest but of practical interest because they were intended not only to guide the research but to find answers relevant to problems most therapists, program managers, and policy makers would like to learn about for enhancing programs and clinical practice. Little is known about pretreatment addiction triggers in the study population. The results of the study may offer specific insights and information that can be of practical benefit to group-treatment therapists who treat women faced with ongoing exposure to addiction relapse triggers.

Definition of Terms

Some terms used in the study can have different meanings. Therefore, for the purposes of clarity, definitions of key terms as they are used within the study are provided. These are not necessarily universally accepted definitions.

Addiction

A complex brain disease characterized by intense (and sometimes uncontrollable) cravings and compulsive seeking of an experience that persists even in the face of devastating consequences (National Institute on Drug Abuse, 2009). Being addicted means giving up conscious control. Addiction is a progressive disease that causes impulsive, unconscious behavior (Dean, 2009).

Addiction Treatment

A broad range of service or prescribe treatments with the overall goal of reducing or eliminating drug use and restoring an addict to productive life (Madigan, 2010).

Relapse

According to chong and Lopez (2008) relapse is defined as any use of alcohol or drugs in the past 30 days at the follow-up points.

First Use

The first time an individual uses any street drug, alcohol or shopping for prescription drugs to self medicate, change mood, thoughts, feelings or to feel fine by any external means.

Qualitative Method

A method of research that uses unstructured information to explore a phenomenon or problem by first trying to understand the problem from the perspective of the party, participant, individual, or group studied. The goal is to try to get as much information as possible about the cause, nature, pattern, and category of the phenomenon or problem from the experience of the individual identified or diagnosed with the problem, through the use of interviews and open questions and answers (Moustakas, 1994). Techniques employed in the process include (a) defining the problem, (b) developing questions to ask, (c) finding a target individual or group, (d) asking open questions regarding the phenomena about which the researcher wants to obtain information, (e) recording or writing down the answers, and (f) storing information for analysis. The end product of qualitative research is a description of the phenomenon and how the data were obtained or analyzed (Moustakas, 1994).

Qualitative methods have been used in drug and alcohol research for organizing and developing an understanding of triggers and relapse. In addition, qualitative methods have been used for studying the impact of drug and alcohol use in the sociocultural context of populations where co-occurring disorders do not exist (Bradizza and Stasiewicz, 2003; Harris, et al., 2005; Smith, 2006; Sterk-Elifson, 1995).

Trigger

Any person, place, thing, or situation that acts as a cue to elicit a craving or desire to use a drug or alcohol or engaging in other addictive behavior (Jaffe, 2010). Such relapse triggers include unpleasant emotions, interpersonal conflict, and social challenges.

ORGANIZATION OF THE BOOK

This book comprises five chapters. In chapter 1 the author introduced the study and presented background information pertaining to addiction and relapse. In chapter 2 the author reviews completed literature review on general addiction, triggers, and specific research involving the effect of general triggers on animals and specific drug and alcohol triggers and women. chapter 3 the author discussed the mixed method approach the researcher used in the study to collect and analyze data. In chapter 4 the author gave report on the result or findings of the study, and chapter 5 the author provided conclusion and recommendations based on the results of the study.

[CHAPTER TWO]

Literature Review

Specific studies on the effects of alcohol and drugs in women are discussed, with limitation of gap in pretreatment addiction triggers. Review of literature shows that the harmful consequences of drug addiction are not sufficient to prevent compulsive drug-seeking and use (National Institute on Drug Abuse, 2010). Being addicted means giving up conscious control. Addiction is a progressive disease that causes impulsive, unconscious behavior (Dean, 2009). Individuals addicted to alcohol, heroin, methamphetamine, marijuana, or prescription drugs become generally dependent on the substance—both physically and psychologically (Drug-Rehabs.org, 2009).

ADDICTIVE DRUGS

Because the researcher assessed drug and alcohol triggers among women with addiction living in the Inland Empire region in Southern California, three of the most common drugs used by this population are discussed in this section, along with their physical effects, to aid the reader's understanding of the experiences reported by the participants in the study.

Prescription Pills Dependence

The overprescribing of approved medical pills is on the rise. Individuals with the money can shop doctors and pharmacies for more prescription pills to cause addictive dependence or alter their mood or feelings of reality.

Methamphetamines

When an individual is under the influence of methamphetamines and high doses are ingested, he or she may become aggressive or violent. Furthermore, there is intense but temporary anxiety resembling panic disorder or generalized anxiety disorder, with paranoid and psychotic features. With higher doses, depressive episodes can occur and may cause legal, family, or relational problems due to the influence of the drug (American Psychiatric Association [APA], 2004). Also, individuals under the influence of methamphetamines can experience altered mental and emotional behavior or exhibit maladaptive behavior.

Cocaine

In regard to cocaine's physical effects, users experience enhanced vigor shortly after use. They also may experience (a) gregariousness, (b) hyperactivity, (c) restlessness, (d) hypervigilance, (e) interpersonal sensitivity, (f) talkativeness, (g) anxiety, (h) tension, (i) alertness, (j) grandiose ideas, (k) anger, (l) impaired judgment, (m) elevated blood pressure, (n) perspiration and chills, (o) psychomotor problems, and (p) respiratory distress, such as chest pain, etc. (APA, 2004).

Alcohol

Alcohol is a generic name for a large group of organic chemical compounds (Boggan, 2008). According to Boggan, an alcoholic beverage is a drink that contains the chemical substance ethanol. Ethanol is the psychoactive constituent in an alcoholic beverage that affects the central nervous system. The effects of alcohol in humans include effects on cognition, behavior, and health.

Alcohol is a central nervous system depressant that produces significant psychoactive effects (Reusch, n.d.). The negative effect of alcohol has generated interest among drug and alcohol counselors, therapists, and law enforcement because of its nature and because it affects both users and nonusers (Boggan, 2008). A study conducted by the Harvard School of Public Health on college binge drinking in the 1990s documented evidence of the impact of alcohol on the behavior and mood of college students (Wechsler, Dowdall, Maener, Gledhill-Hoyt, and Lee, 1998) (see table 1). Califano (2006) examined 15- to 24-year-olds with alcohol-related problems with regard to alcohol-related violence, car crashes, and student deaths. The study shows that individuals with severe drug and alcohol problems failed to attain goals of typical development and psychosocial transition from adolescence to young adulthood, such as marriage, employment, financial independence, and educational attainment.

Table 1

Impact of Drinking Alcohol on the Mood and Behavior of College Students 1993–1997

Impact of drinking alcohol	Proportion of students affected (%)
Had study or sleep interrupted	60.6
Had to take care of a drunken student	50.2
Had been insulted or humiliated	28.6
Driving after drinking	35.8
Had experienced unwanted sexual advances	20.1
Argument with a friend	23.5
Damaged property	10.4
Missed a class	30.2

TRIGGERS

Triggers are elements, tangible things, and intangible thoughts which elicit an automatic response resulting in a return to the addictive pattern (Taylor, 2010). Triggers can be either internal or external in nature (Taylor, 2010). External triggers include specific things that can cause the return to addictive behaviors, such as a particular place, a cigarette, or a specific person (Taylor, 2010). Internal triggers include elements within the body or mind that elicit the return of addictive behavior, such as a physical sensation, emotions, or thoughts (e.g., "I'm not good enough" or "I'm so alone") (Taylor, 2010, p. 64).

According to Connolly, Coffey, Baschnagel, Drobes, and Saladin (2009, p. 2), "Broadly, craving definitions typically focus on subjective urges to perform (negatively or positively) reinforced instrumental and/or conditioned behavior related to the use of addictive substances (e.g., alcohol)."Addolorato, et al., (2005), suggested that craving is multidimensional, corresponding to behavioral, cognitive, and emotional factors. Accordingly, craving triggers a complex mechanism, from which different individuals have "different craving profiles" (Addolorato, et al., 2005, p. 1220).

Triggers can cause stress, sadness, or glee ("Drug Addiction Triggers," 2010). Drug, alcohol, or other substances make addicts feel better at the time of use, and the addicted individual comes to associate those good feelings with the substance. Over time, the addicted person will begin to use the same substance whenever he or she wants to feel better ("Triggers," 2010). The most powerful triggers to avoid are people, places, and emotional triggers such as thought, craving, and uses (USHHS, 2009).

According to the National Institute on Drug Abuse (NIDA), different kinds of triggers exist, including different environmental influences affecting triggers and relapse. A trigger can be anything such as family and friends, socio-community status, peer pressure, physical and sexual abuse, stress, parental involvement, and critical developmental stages in a person's life that will cause or predispose a person to be vulnerable to drug use (National Institute on Drug Abuse, 2010).

The relationship between triggers and behavior was demonstrated in Pavlov's classical conditioning paradigm within the realm of a dog's physiological response. In the experiment performed by Pavlov, the dogs became conditioned to salivate each time the bell rang just before food was served (Carroll, 1998). Later, the dogs were observed and the bell was rung, but no food was served (Carroll, 1998).The dogs continued to demonstrate the salivation response even when the food was not served. Pavlov concluded that the salivation was a conditioned response resulting because the dogs became used to the sound of the bell and associated the food with the conditional cue of the bell (Carroll, 1998).

Similar responses have been observed in the human brain, which also learns to react to conditional stimuli (Pate, 2009). For example, people may experience overwhelming memories and emotions that seem to come out of nowhere when they hear music to which they used to get high, or when they pass by a street where they used to buy drugs or sex (Jaffe, 2010).

Triggers can cause relapse among addicts. A relapse trigger, like the bell in Pavlov's experiment, can be any person, place, thing, or situation that reminds a person of his or her drug and alcohol use (Urell, 2010). Common triggers include being around people with whom one previously used drugs, having money or getting paid, drinking alcohol, social situations, and certain affective states such as anxiety, depression, or joy (Carroll, 1998).

Triggers and Addictive Behavior/Relapse

Addiction is a chronic relapsing disorder characterized by elements of compulsion (results in seeking and taking the drug), loss of control (in terms of ability to limit intake), and negative emotional state (in absence of the drug) (Koob and Le Moal, 2008). According to Koob and Le Moal (2008),"A key of the addiction process is the under activation of natural motivational systems such that the reward system becomes compromised and that an antireward system becomes recruited to provide the powerful motivation for drug seeking associated with compulsive use" (p. 30). The brain reward systems are conceptualized as the activation of the response to positive reinforcement. In contrast, the antireward system is designed to limit rewards triggered by excessive activity of the reward system (Koob and Le Moal, 2008). The addictive state, therefore, involves "a long-term, persistent plasticity in the activity of neural circuits mediating motivational systems that derives from recruitment of antireward systems that drive aversive states" (Koob and Le Moal, 2008, p. 38).

This deregulation of the motivational systems tends to persist during abstinence, despite the length of abstinence, maintaining a persistent vulnerability to relapse triggers and craving via activation of the neurological circuits (Koob and Le Moal, 2008). Koob and Le Moal (2008, p. 38) defined *craving* as, "memory of the rewarding effects of a drug superimposed upon a negative emotional state." *Relapse* is described as "the reinitiating of drug seeking and drug taking after abstinence" (Stewart, 2008, p. 3147). Substance cravings have been found to predict post-treatment relapse (Bottlender and Soyka, 2004; Chong and Lopez, 2008).

According to Stewart, craving and the renewal of drug-seeking behavior after abstinence can be induced by re-exposure to the drug or experience of cues associated by the individual to the drug as well as other experiences of stress (Stewart, 2008). Drug addiction creates long-lasting changes in the brain, forming a vulnerability to relapse from either internal or external triggers. Such changes develop over time with further exposure to the drug, encompassing more regions of the brain with each exposure (Porrino, et al., 2004; Stewart, 2008) and behavioral consequences (Kalivas and O'Brien, 2008).

Within the brain, internal and external triggers are paired with the effects of the drug and thus remain capable of eliciting a drug-seeking response despite long-term abstinence (Stewart, 2008). Although some psychological techniques have been found to reduce reinstatement due to reexposure (in terms of the drug, cues, or stressors), Stewart (2008) stated, "Few are sufficiently broad in their effects to serve as effective treatments" (p. 3154).

Several studies have been done to investigate the relationship between triggers and relapse behaviors among animals and humans. Enkel, Spanagel, Vollmayr, and Schneider (2010) sought to determine whether stress could trigger anhedonic-like behavior in congenitally helpless (cLH) rats, an accepted model of depression. The investigators measured anhedonia by a reduction of sweetened condensed milk (SCM) intake and the pleasure attenuated startle response (PAS) induced by an electric foot-shock stress challenge in group-housed rats.

According to Enkel, et al., (2010), the rats in the study were kept under single-housing conditions, which served as an environmental factor that induced anhedonia-like behavior in genetically predisposed rats. Thirty-two helpless (cLH) rats and 30 rats in the control group, aged 9 to 13 weeks, were used in the study. The rats were kept in a group house in standard Makrolon cages and under standard conditions (12-hour light/dark cycle; lights on at 8:00 a.m.) with water and food available, except on testing days. The animals were maintained on a mild food restriction timetable of 15g lab chow per day. Furthermore, foot-shock stress exposure electric shocks were applied in modified Skinner boxes equipped with a grid floor consisting of twenty-four electrical steel rods and electrical walls. Levels were retracted. After 3 minutes of habituation, four unsignaled shocks (2 s, 0.8 mA, pulsed) were delivered at a variable interstimulus interval (60–30 s).One minute after the last shock, the rats were returned to the home cage. After 5 minutes of habituation, rats had access to the sweetened solution for 15 minutes. The amount of liquid consumed was recorded for each rat and was calculated in relation to the individual body weight (ml/kg). The results of the study showed a reduction in milk intake among the helpless rats with anhedonia, compared with the control rats. In addition, the results showed a decrease in the pleasure-attenuated startle (PAS) response, indicating a deficient reward perception, demonstrating learned helplessness and stress trigger anhedonia-like behavior in congenitally helpless rats. Furthermore, stress shock can decrease milk consumption in rats with learned helplessness (Enkel, et al., 2010). A limitation of the study was that other factors, such as taste, could have affected the rats' intake of milk.

Sociological and Environmental Triggers

What we should know is that specific environmental and social factors may serve as cues for individuals who have completed substance abuse treatment and returned to their previous environment and social circumstances. Rosenbloom (2009) conducted a study on triggers designed to test holiday willpower and drug and alcohol dependence. Holidays are particularly perilous times for those in treatment for alcohol problems. Naltrexone has been suggested as an aid to help avoid alcohol-related problems, but such medications work only if the patients take them. The holidays are the worst time for patients' willpower, so these often dramatically fail (Rosenbloom, 2009). The study showed that patients were reluctant to use available resources to mitigate holiday stress and triggers well before the holiday, resulting in relapse. Rosenbloom (2009) suggested that therapists should proactively recommend naltrexone as an aid to treatment in order to provide extra insurance against relapse rather than have patients lament the challenges after the fact.

Early pubertal maturation, family problems, and poverty are risk factors for drug and alcohol use (Costello, Sung, Worthman, and Angold, 2006; Rosenbloom, 2009). Adolescent substance use and abuse have been linked to a wide range of family and environmental problems (Costello, et al., 2006). Costello, et al., (2006), tested the theory that puberty exacerbates triggers for drug use and relapse. The authors aggregated a large number of risk factors included in the test data set into three categories, using item response modeling and factor analysis. The group labeled "poverty and adversity" included (a) family income below the federal poverty line; (b) parental lack of education; (c) parental unemployment; (d) single, step, and adopted family structure; and (e) multiple moves of home and school. The group labeled "family problems" showed (a) parental history of mental illness, (b) crime, (c) drug problems, and (d) family violence and other risk factors, including childhood psychiatric disorders, life events, and association with deviant peers. Increased levels of testosterone were associated with risks of alcohol use in boys, controlling for age. From age 12 onward, mature boys had higher rates of alcohol risk than did immature boys. Among girls, the interaction was not significant. Mature girls had a higher alcohol risk than immature girls after age 12. The link between early maturation and conduct disorder was seen in girls only. Of maturing girls, 80% had conduct disorder and deviant peers using alcohol. For maturing boys, it was 83%. The increased risk of alcohol use associated with all three risk factors was significant for both boys and girls.

The results of the study by Costello, et al., (2006), demonstrated that family triggers such as early maturity, family poverty, and adversity did not increase the risk of alcohol use in early-maturing boys. Interestingly, poverty marginally decreased the risk of alcohol use among early maturing boys; however, child-rearing style, specifically the lack of adequate supervision, increased the risk of alcohol use for both boys and girls. Family problems increased the risk of alcohol use in early-maturing boys, but the effect on girls, while in the same direction, was not significant.

The impact of early maltreatment (neglect, physical abuse, or sexual abuse) on boys was not a significant trigger, and although girls who had been maltreated reached maturity on average eight months earlier than non-maltreated girls, early maltreatment had no effect on alcohol use in girls. When the interrelation of different family risk factors was tested to predict early alcohol use for early-maturing girls, the results showed that the risk was present and increased for girls. Finally, Costello, et al., concluded that although poverty was a marker for boys in terms of risk for use of alcohol, poverty was not a significant risk factor for girls' use of alcohol.

Other researchers have looked at the relationship between age and drug or alcohol use. Peer drinking and peer acceptance affect a significant number of adolescents and young adults between ages 12 and 20, although drinking under age 21 is illegal (Califano, 2006). Califano (2006) also found that adolescents who start drinking before age 15 are four times more likely to develop alcohol dependence than those who begin drinking at age 21; therefore, by the time an adolescent turns 17 or 18 and is ready for college, he or she may have already developed a drinking problem. Many of the factors present in the early stages may become strong relapse triggers.

Tevyaw, Borsari, Colby, and Monti (2007) designed a study to determine the effectiveness of incorporating peer motivation for decreasing alcohol use among college students mandated to receive treatment after violating campus alcohol policy. In the study, 36 male participants were randomly assigned to receive either two 45-minute sessions of an individual motivational intervention (IMI, n = 18) or a peer-enhanced motivational intervention (PMI, n = 18). The IMI variables included (a) exploration of motivation to change alcohol use, (b) perceived negative effect of drinking, (c) personalized feedback, and (d) goals for changing alcohol consumption and related behaviors. The PMI variables included all elements or variables of the IMI plus the presence of a supportive peer of the participants during both sessions. The results provided by Tevyaw, et al., (2007), showed that the magnitude of within-group reduction in alcohol use and problems was three times larger on average for the PMI than for the IMI group. Therefore, the findings reported by Tevyaw, et al., showed promise for the inclusion of peers' in brief motivational intervention for mandated students as a future strategy for reducing alcohol behaviors.

The limitation of the study by Tevyaw, et al., (2007), is that it failed to take into account environmental problems and predisposing factors that may contribute to drinking behavior and drunkenness among college students. The usefulness of the study is that peer influence could help decrease alcohol use if included in treatment intervention.

PROBLEMS IN DRUG AND ALCOHOL TREATMENT

According to the literature, current addiction treatment refers to a broad range of services provided to people suffering from addiction. These services include identification, intervention, assessment, diagnosis, counseling, health care, psychiatric services, psychological services, social services, and follow-up procedures. The overall goal of treatment is to reduce or eliminate drug use and restore the addict to productive life (Madigan, 2010). The experience and compulsion to get drugs, take drugs, and experience the effect of drugs has dominated their every waking moment, and drug abuse has taken the place of all the things they used to enjoy doing (NIDA, 2010). Also, drug addiction is associated with other social problems including neglect or complete elimination of important activities like work, school, or social contact when under the influence.

To develop effective pretreatment relapse intervention, the clinician must understand what pretreatment addiction treatment is. The environment of an addict may be a major contributing factor in relapse behaviors. Environmental triggers include but are not limited to different influences, from family and friends to socio-community status, quality of life in general, peer pressure, physical and sexual abuse, stress and parental involvement.

QUALITATIVE RESEARCH METHODS FOR CLINICIANS

Qualitative research has been used in many studies to understand the relationship between trigger and relapse. It is important to review the benefits of qualitative research methods for two reasons: first, to understand the general principles and methods; and second, to understand the application of qualitative methods in the present study of pretreatment addiction triggers among women with addiction disorders.

Qualitative research produces findings not obtained by statistical procedures or other means of quantification (Neill, 2009). Qualitative research has been used in the past to study phenomena such as triggers of drug use. By virtue of their training, knowledge, and exposure to the population or situation in question, practicing clinicians will have already made some sense of the phenomenon to be studied from their own experience. Therefore, instead of constructing theories from scratch, as researchers new to the field must do, researching clinicians must (a) face their previous constructions (sense-making from experience), (b) create methods that allow for deconstruction (sense-making challenged), and then (c) work towards building reconstructions (sense-making remade) (Chenail and Maione, 1997).

Qualitative research methods become useful in this respect when used by researcher or clinicians to reflect on one observation at a time and use a new sense-making perspective to look for something qualitatively different in the phenomenon from what is known and from what had been the focus of study (Chenail and Maione, 1997). Qualitative research creates an atmosphere for developing an understanding of individuals' situations or problems prior to the change factor or prior to the time skills are applied.

How has the qualitative method been applied in female alcohol and drug research? Patton (2002) explained why a qualitative analysis approach is a useful tool for analyzing addiction triggers present before an addict relapsed and experienced the side effects associated with drug use. Whether quantitative research data are more desirable, valid, or meaningful than qualitative self-reported data is not at issue. Although review of the literature on relapse triggers can be useful, it is even more useful to have addicted individuals' document their experience. Although therapists cannot observe their clients' specific triggers before relapse, arrest, and referral to treatment, it is important to learn about addicts' thoughts and behavior before and after they became addicted. Recognizing the thought patterns and behavior associated with addiction helps all stakeholders involved in treatment to go behind closed doors into the world of secrets (Chenail and Maione, 1997). Qualitative methodologies are powerful tools for enhancing our understanding of a phenomenon such as unobserved addiction triggers (Hoepfl, 1997).

Qualitative Analysis of Addiction

Qualitative methods have been used in drug and alcohol research for developing an understanding of triggers and relapse and for studying the impact of drug and alcohol use in a sociocultural context (Sterk-Elifson, 1995). Sterk-Elifson (1995) examined changes in drug use patterns and the impact of drug use patterns on women's lives and on related issues such as support of the drug habit and setting of use. The project was called "Project Fast," and the duration of the study was from June 1992 through June 1994. The researchers used in-depth interviews of the women, supplemented by ethnographic or social mapping, including participant observation, with the researchers visiting the women in different neighborhoods and interviewing them (Sterk-Elifson, 1995). The criteria used to determine eligibility for the study were that a woman had to live in the Atlanta metropolitan area, be 18 years of age or older, and be an active drug user. "Active drug user" was defined as injecting on at least four days per week during the last year (Sterk-Elifson, 1995). Crack cocaine users had to use at least three grams of cocaine per week or have used daily during the last year (Sterk-Elifson, 1995). A total of 164 female drug users participated in the study and were interviewed about topics such as family background, reproduction history, drug use and drug treatment experience, violence, abuse, and health history, including HIV and AIDS. In addition to the interview data, a focus group provided another level of analysis and consensus building. Rather than forming a process group, Sterk-Elifson (1995) conducted in-depth interviews, supplemented by ethnographic contact with the addicts. Qualitative measures included characteristics such as self-esteem and knowledge of HIV and AIDS.

Women in the focus groups discussed and provided insight into their triggers and experiences. The data revealed the triggers, behaviors, and patterns of drug use among the women in the Atlanta area who participated in the study. The results were critical for understanding substance abuse patterns and for developing intervention strategies to minimize potential harm from drug use to the users, users' communities, and society at large (Sterk-Elifson, 1995).

Qualitative Analysis of Recovery, Relapse, and Prevention

Many factors contribute to relapse after recovery, including genetic factors, changes in neurons and neurotransmitter function from heavy drug use, and the continuance of these changes within the brain after cessation of use, enabling environmental cues to trigger craving and relapse. It is necessary for any method designed to prevent or minimize relapses to consider the individual triggers and stressors (Kelly, et al., 2007). Kelly, et al., reported:

> Relapses are not sudden events that fall out of the blue. Patients need to learn the chains of events and behaviors that lead to their relapses. Triggers and stresses are often highly individual. They must be identified in each person in order to help him or her learn to prevent or minimize relapses. (p. 381)

Harris, Fallot, and Berley (2005) used qualitative semistructured interviews to examine elements of sustained recovery among women with co-occurring disorders who had survived trauma, with a focus on substance abuse recovery. They asked 27 women to describe the most significant factors in both sustaining and hindering their recovery. Harris, et al., identified seven themes in the factors that sustained or hindered the recovery of participants; four of these were supportive and three served as obstacles to recovery. Connection, self-awareness, a sense of purpose and meaning, and spirituality were the supportive themes revealed through the analysis, whereas battles with depression and despair, destructive habits and patterns, and lack of personal control were revealed as themes that were obstacles to recovery.

Smith (2006) explored chronic sorrow as a relapse trigger for female substance abusers with a history of child abuse enrolled in a substance abuse treatment program. Smith used qualitative measures to describe the participants' feelings and experiences related to their relapse. According to Smith, 12 women participated in semi structured interviews to explore their perceptions of relapse. The findings of the study revealed three common themes: (a) mothering loss, (b) blocking feelings, and (c) relapse triggers. Participants suggested the use of interpersonal reflection as well as cognitive and action-based coping skills as a means of avoiding relapse.

Psychosocial interventions characteristically maintain a focus on both abstinence and personal and social coping mechanisms (Kelly, et al., 2007). Cognitive-behavioral therapy (Beck, 1993) emphasizes the patient's understanding of his or her false beliefs (cognitive element) that may have precipitated the substance use and abuse; with this understanding, the patient can change the way he or she deals with the craving to avoid using the addictive substance (behavioral element). The therapist works with the patient to employ behavioral changes to avoid the addictive behavioral response (Kelly, et al., 2007).

Motivational interviewing (Miller and Rollnick, 2009) is a method in which the therapist leads the addict through several stages of change. According to Miller and Rollnick (2009), "Motivational interviewing is described as a collaborative, person-centered form of guidance designed to elicit and strengthen motivation for change" (p.137). The stages range from unawareness of the need for change from substance dependence, to a realization of the need to change, taking action to change behaviors, and finally, maintaining behavioral changes. The therapist focuses on the individual's personal motivations for change and incorporates them into the behavioral change implementation plan. Within this strategy, relapse is accepted as possible, yet not a failure. Instead, a relapse signals the need to move backward in the stages, without erosion of the individual's self-efficacy (Kelly, et al., 2007).

The development of an acceptance-based coping intervention designed to prevent alcohol dependency relapse was presented by Vieten, et al., (2010), who contended that negative affect serves as a common relapse trigger after successful treatment for alcohol dependency. Vieten, et al., presented an intervention strategy unique from the change-based strategies commonly used for managing a negative effect (or cognitions), termed "acceptance-based coping for relapse prevention (ABCRP)." It was proposed by the authors as a new intervention designed to treat alcohol-dependent individuals within the first six months of initial and continued abstinence from drinking. The study revealed improvements in self-reported negative affect, emotional reactivity, stress, positive affect, well-being, mindfulness and awareness, and reduction in craving.

Using focus group data, Bradizza and Stasiewicz (2003) analyzed high-risk drug and alcohol use situations among severely mentally ill substance abusers, illustrating the use of a qualitative study in understanding relapse triggers, patterns, and behavior. According to Bradizza and Stasiewicz, situational factors have been found to influence relapse to alcohol and drug use in general samples of abuse, but little previous research existed that examined the influence of interpersonal and intrapersonal determinants in samples of individuals dually diagnosed with severe mental illness and substance use disorders. Bradizza and Stasiewicz obtained qualitative data from the participants regarding the types of high-risk alcohol and drug use situations they most often encountered in their daily lives. This study represents the first known effort to assess high-risk situations in severe mental illness. The authors developed taxonomy of relapse episodes based on interviews with abusers who emphasized a situational analysis of potential relapse episodes. Relapse episodes were classified into one of eight types of intrapersonal or interpersonal situations. The intrapersonal situations included unpleasant emotional states, pleasant emotions, physical discomfort, testing personal control, and urges or temptations to use. The interpersonal situations included conflict with others, social pressure to use, and pleasant times with others.

In the Bradizza and Stasiewicz (2003) study, data were collected from patient charts as well as from a focus group discussion. The medical charts were reviewed at the clinic, and information was obtained regarding demographic variables, mental health, substance abuse diagnosis, and psychiatric medication. The group data were taped, rather than handwritten or typed, and later transcribed for analysis. Participants (21 women and 20 men) were diagnosed primarily with a psychotic disorder or a recurrent major affective disorder. Participants were recruited from two dual-diagnosis outpatient programs in the Buffalo, New York, area. The group composition was 75% African American, 19% Caucasian, and 6% Hispanic; 72% were single or never married, 25% were separated or divorced, and 3% were married or cohabiting. Participants had a mean of 11.3 years of education, and 94% were currently unemployed. Fifty-five percent had a major affective disorder diagnosis (44% major depression, 8% bipolar, 3% dysthymia), and 45% had a psychotic disorder diagnosis (22% schizophrenia, 17%

schizoaffective, 6% psychotic disorder NOS). Antipsychotic medication was being prescribed for 97% of participants.

Bradizza and Stasiewicz (2003) described the data collection process for the study as follows: The group was asked questions about difficulties in handling everyday situations; questions focused on alcohol and drug use. The group session began with questions regarding general social situations the participants found difficult to manage. Group members were also asked about high-risk situations or triggers for substance abuse. Participants were required to attend one of ten 75-minute audio-taped sessions. The groups were small, with only 6 to 12 individuals, and the sessions were facilitated by a group moderators.

The data obtained were divided into two parts: numbers and descriptive statistics were used to analyze the quantitative demographic and diagnostic information obtained from the chart review, and qualitative data were analyzed through the use of a multilevel process that focused on the classification of responses related to high risk during an alcohol use situation. Themes were extracted from the data, with the results showing a consensus of 10 themes encompassing a total of 33 high-risk situations. These themes included both interpersonal and intrapersonal situations. The study demonstrated that qualitative research techniques offer insight into understanding the behavior of participants and provide a valuable foundation for further quantitative study. The study also showed that individuals with severe mental illness can participate in semistructured focus groups.

Gerwe (2000) performed an in-depth case study of 30 patients in an outpatient addiction treatment program to study the concept of negative emotional state and its relation to drug relapse using the high-risk identification and prediction treatment model (HRIPTM). This model was used to explore the nature of repetitive negative behavior patterns, the nature of negative emotional states, and the subsequent influence of these factors on addiction and susceptibility to addiction/relapse. Gerwe described addiction as a developmental process and therefore highlighted the importance of identification of lifetime experiences that are associated or connected to the addictive behaviors, the internal and emotional factors associated with the behaviors, and the associated risk for each individual. Understanding the mentality and behavior associated with addiction could help everyone involved in treatment gain knowledge that exists behind closed doors and find unobserved pretreatment relapse triggers within a world of secrets and addictions (Chenail and Maione, 1997).

[CHAPTER THREE]
Methodology

Many women with addiction disorders who are referred by the courts for drug and alcohol treatment or released after treatment into the community are exposed on a daily basis to the same cues that triggered addictive behavior before they entered treatment. Understanding these triggers would enhance treatment programs, because having information available to explain the causes, patterns, and categories of addiction triggers would enable therapists to target responses to specific triggers in order to improve their group treatment and support programs and to prevent relapse. Unfortunately, no data on pretreatment triggers are available for use in planning treatment specific to women with addiction disorders in the Inland Empire region. To help overcome this limitation, methods are needed to enable assessment of triggers that influence addictive behavior in this population.

According to Patton (2002), inquiry strategies, measurement approaches, and analysis procedures can be mixed and matched in the search for relevant and useful methods for assessing pretreatment triggers. In the present study, the researcher used mixed method research including a qualitative case-study design supported by descriptive statistics to explore the experiences and perceptions of women with a history of drug and alcohol abuse. The researcher used a survey instrument including open-ended questions to gather information. The data were analyzed through a case-study analysis incorporating content analysis techniques.

RESEARCH QUESTIONS

Data collected in the study were reported and analyzed for each of the four research questions:

1. How do women with addiction disorders who live in the Inland Empire region experience triggers of addiction relapse?
2. What are the contributing factors, patterns, and categories of addiction relapse triggers experienced by these women?
3. Are relapse triggers the same as the triggers of an individual's initial drug use?
4. What is perceived to be the most effective way for individuals in the Inland Empire community to respond to addiction relapse triggers?

RESEARCH METHOD AND DESIGN

The researcher utilized a mixed method in this study. A qualitative case study design was used to assess pre-treatment relapse triggers among women with addiction disorders who live in the Inland Empire region. The qualitative data were supported by quantitative data obtained from scaled questions on the survey served to support the qualitative findings through descriptive statistics. The participants were given a questionnaire and were asked to rate and describe their trigger experiences.

What we should know is that qualitative studies are not generally used to test hypotheses or examine preset variables or aspects of the investigation; rather, qualitative studies seek to reveal themes of research through an inductive rather than deductive process (Creswell, 2009). In the case of this study, in which the data consisted of the reported experiences, beliefs, and truths of women with addiction disorders, no hypotheses could be made with regard to specific relapse triggers before themes emerging from the data could be identified to support a specific theory. In addition, the quantitative portion of the study used descriptive statistics for rating scale data to further identify and illustrate the perceptions and experiences of participants, rather than correlation or predictive statistics; therefore, the development of hypotheses was not appropriate in this study.

Research Methods

A mixed qualitative and quantitative method was selected for this study because mixed-method research offered several benefits, including opportunities to explore lived experiences of participants while quantifying the perceived scale of influence of certain triggers and other related factors on the individual experience of addiction and/or relapse (Creswell, 2007, 2009). Qualitative research is the exploration of multiple meanings—socially and historically constructed—of individual experiences in order to develop a theory or pattern (Creswell, 2007, 2009). Qualitative studies focus on the importance of the participant's perspective and the way it informs the personal meaning held by the participant (Creswell, 2007, 2009). The qualitative method also provides flexibility in exploring a subject, while allowing an in-depth investigation, potentially leading to the development of a new observation and the opportunity for further exploration of prevalence, predictors, and sequence in other studies (Yoshikawa, Weisner, Kalil, and Way, 2008). Qualitative methods are inquiry-based, enabling the exploration of an occurrence through questions, narrative descriptions, and analysis of emerging themes (Creswell, 2005). Qualitative methods provided a representation of the specific focus of the study, based on the interpretation of lived experiences of the participants (Creswell, 2005; Neuman, 2003). The forms of data collection in qualitative studies can include observations, interviews, questionnaires, documents, and audiovisual materials (Creswell, 2005).

Patton (2002) explained why a qualitative approach might be useful for analyzing pretreatment trigger experiences. Patton (2002) stated that the issue is not whether observational data are more desirable, valid, or meaningful than self-reported data; therapists cannot observe what individuals have done in their pretreatment addiction phase and lifestyle before coming for help or treatment. Qualitative research has a focus on the detail and depth of information received from a relatively small population, which provides a rich and detailed understanding, whereas quantitative research provides the ability to form broad generalizations from a specific population (Patton, 2002).

The researcher used a quantitative method for the analysis of the perceived level of significance of various triggers, the strength of conviction and motivation of the participants to remain sober. The quantitative method was a Likert rating scale for survey questions. This method provided the researcher with the ability to assess and compare numerical data from the rating scales (Cozby, 2007).

Mixed-method research relies on both quantitative and qualitative methods that are consequences-oriented, problem-centered, and pluralistic (Creswell, 2009). According to Morrow (2007), qualitative research is also appropriate when one needs to present a detailed and in-depth view of a phenomenon. Whereas quantitative methods can enable the researcher to get a broad understanding of a phenomenon, qualitative approaches are able to delve into complex processes and illustrate the multifaceted nature of a human phenomenon.

The researcher designed the study to explore in detail the pretreatment trigger experience of women with a history of addiction and vulnerability to relapse. Therefore, a mixed qualitative and quantitative method approach was appropriate for the study.

Research Design

In working out a design for the study, the goal was to find a strategy that would provide the most useful information for understanding pre-treatment relapse triggers among women with addition disorders. According to Patton (2002), if individuals or groups are the primary unit of analysis, then case studies of people or groups may be the focus for research. Thus, the qualitative therapeutic approach used in the current study was a descriptive case study design. The case study design is a common method for developing a theory, evaluating programs, and developing interventions for existing programs because it allows researchers to reveal and understand multifaceted phenomena (Baxter and Jack, 2008). Case study theory is based on a constructivist paradigm (Stake, 1995).

A case study research approach is useful for studies that have unknown variables, use interviews and observation, and have flexible guidelines (Creswell, 2005). Because the current study was exploratory in nature, it lent itself to the use of case study methods to assess the potential for identification and understanding of pretreatment triggers. Researchers' generally use case studies when they are concerned with gathering real-life data from participants and creating an understanding of a specific phenomenon (Yin, 1994). Thus, the case study design was well suited for exploring and reporting on the experiences and perceptions of relapse triggers in women with addiction disorders in the Inland Empire region.

An advantage of case study research is the close collaboration between the researcher and the participants (Baxter and Jack, 2008). Through this collaboration, the participants can describe their views of reality, thus providing researchers with a better understanding of the phenomenon and participant actions (Lather, 1992). In addition, case studies are useful because they allow researchers to use both quantitative and qualitative methods to examine the data (Yin, 2009). Case study theory enables researchers to answer questions such as "why" or "how" while being able to consider the influence of the context of a phenomenon (Baxter and Jack, 2008).

According to Stake (1995), case study design, "ensures topic of interest is well explored and that the essence of the phenomenon is revealed" (p.10). Case studies explore situations in which the topic being evaluated has no clear, single set of outcomes (Yin, 2009). A case study design was appropriate for the current study because the goal of the study was to answer these "how" and "why" questions without manipulating the behavior of participants (Yin, 2009).

Consistent with the goal of developing a mixed design for the study, the survey instrument used yielded both qualitative and quantitative data. The qualitative data obtained from the open-ended questions were collected and analyzed using some of the techniques described by Yin (2009), including pattern matching, explanation building, and cross-case synthesis. The quantitative data from the survey were analyzed using descriptive statistics. Within a descriptive study, the primary goal of the quantitative analysis is to "characterize a population or process based on certain attributes in that population or process" (Ott and Longnecker, 2010, p. 19). Therefore, quantitative descriptive statistics were used to examine the Likert scale items on the survey.

The qualitative design of phenomenology was considered for this study, but was deemed less appropriate, as the design would not enable the incorporation of quantitative data. Although phenomenology has a focus on exploration and description of the lived experiences of participants (Creswell, 2009; Moustakas, 1994), the phenomenological design would not have covered all aspects of the study goals, which were not only to explore the perceptions and experiences of the participants, but also to examine quantitative measures of elements related to addiction and relapse via a Likert rating scale. Incorporation of both qualitative and quantitative methods allowed for a broader and more complete picture of the perceived relative importance of various elements to the addiction and relapse experiences of individuals.

POPULATION AND SAMPLING

The researcher employed a purposeful sampling plan. Purposeful sampling is a nonrandom sampling method in which the researcher selects particular research locations and participants to increase the probability that they will be able to provide the information necessary to answer the research questions of the study (Creswell, 2005). Selecting qualitative samples focuses on a collection of participants who provide specific narratives to clarify and deepen the exploration of the study (Neuman, 2003).

Quantitative research typically calls for larger sample sizes (over 30) (Ott and Longnecker, 2010), whereas qualitative research normally involves small samples of participants (Creswell, 2005). Although Creswell (2005) recommended that the size of a qualitative sample should range from 1 to 25 participants, and Polkinghorne (2005) recommended 5 to 25 participants, Patton (2002) stated that there are no specific rules for sample size: "Sample size depends on what you want to know, the purpose of the inquiry, what's at stake, what will be useful, what will have credibility, and what can be done with available time and resources" (p. 244).

Study Population

In the current study, the researcher explored the perceptions and lived experiences of women with addiction disorders in the Inland Empire region. Therefore, the goal was to select the research sample from the population of women with drug or alcohol addiction disorders who resided in the Inland Empire region. The sample size was based on the overall need to provide an in-depth analysis and the expected availability of participants. Eligibility criteria for the study were as follows: female sex, resident of the Inland Empire region at the time of the study, resident of a shelter/treatment facility located in downtown San Bernardino city, (the treatment facility has been deleted from the report) with history of drug or alcohol addiction, and age between 18 and 50 years. Participation was voluntary.

A total of 22 women participated in the study. They had come from towns and cities in Inland Empire, and all were residents of a treatment facility at the time of the study. All had a history of addiction but no specific diagnosis was obtained including use of methamphetamine, amphetamine (speed), cocaine, alcohol, or marijuana as their drug of choice. The participants ranged in age from 17 to 45 years. The seventeen-year-old was a mother with the ability to make independent decisions and who met the requirements for consenting to participate in the study. The majority of the participants had attended high school and could read, respond to questions and write.

Informed Consent and Confidentiality

Since this study involves direct participants participation participants were assured confidentiality. Confidentiality is the process of holding participants' personal information in confidence without disclosure to the public (Neuman, 2003). Therefore, the study did not include or ask for specific personal identifying information about the participants. Thus, no individual identifiable data were collected (for example, last name, address, employer, names of relatives, date of birth, telephone number, e-mail address, Social Security number, account information, voice print, fingerprint, photos, personal chart information [including codes and diagnoses], or any other characteristic that may identify an individual). Participant confidentiality was maintained through the use of pseudonyms for each participant, rather than personal identifiable information.

The data consisted of anonymized individual responses obtained from the survey. Because there was no possibility of identifying individual participants' problems or responses, disclosure of responses for the study analysis would not place participants in criminal or civil liability, damage their financial standing, employability, or reputation, or break confidentiality required by law or federal or institutional regulation.

INSTRUMENTATION

The survey instrument for this study was a questionnaire that included a set of Likert rating scale items as well as a set of open-ended questions for description of trigger experiences (appendix A). The questions were contained in a questionnaire booklet designed for this study and ready for distribution. Treatment center staff members administered the questionnaire and provided appropriate care in case an individual exhibited flashback or distress when answering questions. In such an event, staff members followed emergency protocol as defined in center's policy for working with individuals with addiction disorders.

DATA COLLECTION

The researcher obtained written permission to conduct the research among women affected by drug use and relapse. The researcher then distributed an informed consent form .The consent form identified the purpose of the study; explained the requirements for participation, risks and benefits, confidentiality of data, conditions for withdrawal; and asked for the volunteer's signature.

The data collected consisted of the participants' responses to the questionnaire described above, which contained both Likert rating scale items and open-ended survey questions. The questionnaire was expected to take approximately 20 to 30 minutes to complete.

No payments were given to individuals for participating in the study. Special precautions were established to protect the confidentiality of the responses, as described above. The major foreseeable risk to the participants was the possibility of an emotional crisis due to recollection of unpleasant feelings associated with a trigger. Staff from the shelter was available to provide crisis support while the participants were completing the questionnaire.

The researcher stored the data in a secure file for analysis. As mentioned in the section on confidentiality above, the data did not include or contain personal identifying information (name, address, employer, names of relatives, date of birth, telephone number, e-mail address, Social Security number, voice print, fingerprint, photos, personal chart information [including codes and diagnoses], or any other identifying characteristics). Individuals were asked to share general biographical data, excluding those listed above. The researcher used the information gained from the data obtained from the questionnaire to develop a descriptive understanding of the problem of pretreatment triggers of addictive behavior experienced by this population (Moustakas, 1994).

Specific Procedures for Collecting Data

7/30/11   The researcher went to the treatment facility to go over plans to administer the questionnaire, the instructions to be given to participants on 8/1/11, and to ensure staff availability to respond to any sudden emergency. Participants who wanted to participate picked-up the questionnaire.

8/1/11   The questionnaire was handed to 15 participants on 8/1/11 with instructions for responding to the questions. About 15 to 20 minutes were used for filling out the responses. Treatment facility staff members collected the filled-out questionnaires and stored them in the brown envelope.

8/1/11   The researcher arrived at the treatment facility to pick up the brown envelope containing the participants' responses.

8/15/11   The same procedures were repeated with 7 additional participants, and the responses were again picked up by the researcher for analysis.

No incidents were reported during the study.

DATA ANALYSIS

In descriptive case study framework, the essence of what the participants conveyed was extracted from the questionnaire and analyzed in order to provide the nature, characteristics, and experiences of addiction triggers. In addition, a theory was generated, serving to demonstrate the nature of addiction triggers specific to this population, which may allow for better treatment options and strategies targeted at relapse triggers for this population.

The case study researcher is concerned with both individual responses as well as the interaction between responses (Yin, 1994). There are four stages that must be executed in order to develop a valid and reliable case study (Yin, 1994). The study was developed according to the four stages as presented by Yin (1994).

The first three stages in designing the case study protocol include (a) the identification of the skills required and to review the protocol; (b) the application of the recommended procedures, including identifying the type of research questions, establishing the degree of control the researcher exerts upon the study parameters, and the scope of focus of the study; and (c) conducting the case study through data collection and conducting interviews/group discussions (1994). The fourth stage in designing a case study is analyzing the evidence that was gathered (Yin, 1994). This stage consists of examining, categorizing, tabulating, and combining the data to develop patterns and themes. Once the data have been analyzed, it is possible to present explanations for the results as well as implications for another research and ways in which the findings apply to other larger areas of interest or society as a whole (Yin, 1994).

Qualitative Data Analysis

The analysis of the case study data followed Merriam's recommendations regarding grouping codes according to content (Merriam, 1998). First, information gathered from the survey employed axial coding (the process of relating codes to each other, via a combination of inductive and deductive reasoning). Next, each occurrence was compared with an occurrence in the same set or in a different set. These initial comparisons led to the development of categories. Comparisons were continually made until all categories were established. The revealed themes were then further categorized; yielding the different perceived elements central to the phenomenon. The final step was a comprehensive review of the data and interpretation of the data to provide the conclusions of the analysis.

The coding categories were created with the assistance of NVivo8 qualitative coding software, which assisted in the coding, categorization, and frequency determination of categories within the transcribed textual data, allowing for the transformation of the data into theoretical groups that can in turn be used to build constructs and theory. Coding software is suggested as a helpful tool for coding qualitative data because the software helps to organize and create meaning within the complex data collected during a qualitative research project (Hunter, Hari, Egbu, and Kelly, 2005). Therefore, NVivo8 qualitative analysis software was used in order to assist in the coding and the development of themes and patterns from the data. NVivo8 software was designed to manage qualitative data by classifying, sorting, and arranging information, and noting the frequency and location of occurrences.

Quantitative Data Analysis

Descriptive statistics were used to describe the Likert scale data obtained from the survey. The data were presented according to descriptive statistics of frequency, mode, median, mean, and variances. The various means were provided as a measure of a central tendency along with the associated percentile and variance. In addition, demographic data were obtained from the participants in terms of gender, age, education, town of origin, choice of drug used, age first used, past drug treatments, and last time clean. These data were used to triangulate the data obtained from the survey processes by demonstrating consistency of the data obtained (qualitative themes uncovered in the analysis and quantitative tendencies) across these demographic variables.

ASSUMPTIONS

The theoretical assumption for this study held that individuals that seek drug and alcohol treatment or sent to treatment after arrest are affected by unknown a pre-treatment relapsed triggers and experiences that dominate their lives. The unknown in the mind of the individual in treatment holds the cues or triggers that can affect the progress of drug use or relapse. Thus, it was very important to tap into that unknown experience base prior to reaching out into existing evidence-based descriptive information. Individuals, therapists, and loved ones should first avail themselves of the unknown and unobserved reality of relapse experience in order to be effective in processing and planning intervention. It was assumed that knowing this experience-based information would help the clinician to understand realities from a descriptive phenomenon, identify and reduce conflict, and increase cooperation and interest through meaning, recognition, and exchange.

VALIDITY AND RELIABILITY

Validity is based on determining whether the findings are accurate at the standpoint of the researcher, the participant, or the readers of an account, whereas reliability evidenced that the approach can be consistent across different researchers and projects (Creswell, 2005, 2007). Validity and reliability of the study were enhanced by the incorporation of the process of member checking (Creswell, 2005), where in addicted individuals had access to read the outcome or report of the analysis for feedback.

Yin (1994) suggested reporting a detailed protocol for data collection so that the procedure of a qualitative study might be replicated in another setting. Therefore, in order to ensure reliability of the study, the collection of data followed the procedure described in the previous data analysis section. Qualitative validity was also improved using NVivo8 qualitative analysis software (QSR International, Melbourne, Australia) to aid in the coding and categorization of the data. Although the researcher conducted the coding and categorization of the data, the software program allowed the researcher to attach codes to the text data from the surveys, as well as search for codes and regroup coded content, while maintaining the integrity of the data (i.e., not breaking up the source data by coded text/content). Use of the qualitative software provided a system to reduce human notation error and maintaining sources of information or textual data because the software tagged all coded data with source information automatically.

CONCLUSION

Chapter 3 discussed the research methodology and design for the study, including a rationale for the design. The current study employed a mixed-method descriptive case study research design. Furthermore, chapter 3 has provided a description of the data collection and analysis processes. The findings of the analysis were used for understanding the pretreatment addiction relapse triggers among a population of individuals from the Inland Empire region of Southern California as well as used to identify and plan intervention to treat pretreatment addiction triggers to prevent relapse. Chapter 4 presents the findings and results of the analysis, and chapter 5 presents the conclusions.

CHAPTER FOUR

Results

The researcher selected mixed method case study research to explore addiction relapse triggers experienced by women with addiction disorders in the Inland Empire region and responses to these triggers that the women perceived to be the most effective. A survey instrument was administered to a sample of 22 women from a single treatment home in the Inland Empire region. The survey consisted of demographic questions, Likert scale questions, and open-ended questions used to collect data that served to identify and describe addiction patterns, causes and triggers, treatment, and relapse. Data obtained from the survey administration were analyzed as described in chapter 3. As such, quantitative data were analyzed using descriptive statistics, with the assistance of SPSS statistical software; qualitative data were analyzed using case study data analysis procedures, as outlined by Merriam (1998).The information gained from this study helps to understand addiction triggers among this population and serves to assist treating and planning intervention to prevent relapse and to improve program focus.

RESEARCH QUESTIONS

This study explored the following research questions:

1. How do women with addiction disorders who live in the Inland Empire region experienced addiction pre-treatment relapse triggers?
2. What are the contributing factors, patterns, and categories of addiction relapse triggers experienced by these women?
3. Are relapse triggers the same as the triggers of an individual's initial drug use?
4. What is perceived to be the most effective way for individuals in the Inland Empire community to respond to addiction relapse triggers?

SUMMARY OF DATA CODING AND ANALYSIS

To answer the stated research question, a mixed method case study analysis was conducted using survey data from a sample of addicted females in Inland Empire. The focus of the study was to understand the experiences and perceptions of these women in order to shed light on the specific causes, patterns, treatment, triggers, and relapse among this population. The data were used to develop a theory on relapse triggers and the influence of various factors on individual risk for relapse. To explore the qualitative data in the form of open-ended questions on the survey instrument, a case study analysis process (Merriam, 1998) was used. In addition, quantitative data obtained from scaled questions on the survey were examined using statistical procedures.

The analysis process included the coding of open-ended survey to identify open coding categories, which then aided in the formation of selective coding categories. The selective coding categories were related to the central theme that emerged from the findings. Accordingly, a narrative was created from the various selective coding categories that served to describe the interrelationships of these categories to the central phenomenon, addiction triggers. Results from the statistical analyses are also presented.

FINDINGS

The quantitative data are presented first, providing a descriptive look at the demographic characteristics of the sample as well as the responses of the sample to the quantitative, scaled questions related to staying sober and the perceived effects of various factors such as familial, financial, social, personal factors on addiction and/or relapse.

Table 2

Demographic Characteristics of Participants (n = 18)

Characteristic	n
Age	
17	1
21–25	4
26–30	5
31–35	6
36–40	1
41–45	1
Education	
Some high school	10
High school graduate	1
Some college	5
Associate degree	2
Ethnicity	
African American	1
Hispanic	7
Asian	2
Caucasian	6
Other	1
No response	1

Quantitative Data

Quantitative data were obtained from survey demographic questions and eleven Likert scale items on the survey. Frequencies and descriptive statistics were used to analyze the quantitative data obtained. Demographic data serve to provide characteristics of the sample. Demographic data collected included gender, age, education, and ethnicity. All participants were women. Table 2 provides further demographic characteristics of the sample.

In addition, the survey collected data related to participant addiction history. This data included the participants' age at first use, number of drug-related arrests, last time they were clean, drug of choice, and whether they had previously participated in addiction treatment. Table 3 illustrates the frequency data for these variables.

Table 3

Participant Addiction History (n = 18)

Variable	n
Age at first use	
7	1
13	3
14	4
16	2
17	2
18	1
21	1
No response	4

(continued)

Table 4

Participant Addiction History (n = 18) (continued)

Variable	n
Number of arrests	
0	11
1	4
10	1
No response	2
Last clean	
Present	3
6–11 months	3
1–2 years	2
3–5 years	1
10+ years	3
N/A or no response	6
Drug of choice	
Meth	7
Alcohol	6
Marijuana	5
Speed	2
Participated in previous treatment	7

The researcher also gathered data in the form of eleven Likert scale questions that were designed to reveal participants' perceptions of their own strength regarding the decision to remain clean; present environment; personal motivation to stay sober; perceived effects of family problems, financial problems, and social problems including events, holidays, as well as the desire/impulse to feel good or to get high as a cause for drug use, addiction, or relapse. Table 5 provides frequency data as well as descriptive statistics on each of the variables of the survey related to the perceived causes of addiction and relapse.

Table 5

Causes of Drug Use (n = 18)

Statistic	Family problems	Financial problems	People/friends	Events	Holidays	Desire to feel good	Desire to feel high
n valid	16	17	18	18	17	17	16
M	3.19	3.29	2.89	2.56	2.76	3.00	2.38
SE	.430	.400	.419	.354	.398	.364	.340
SD	1.721	1.649	1.779	1.504	1.640	1.500	1.360
Frequency of rating, n (%)							
1	5 (28)	4 (22)	6 (33)	6 (33)	6 (33)	4 (22)	5 (28)
2	0	1 (6)	4 (22)	4 (22)	2 (11)	2 (11)	5 (28)
3	4 (22)	5 (28)	0	3 (17)	3 (17)	5 (28)	3 (17)
4	1 (6)	0	2 (11)	2 (11)	2 (11)	2 (11)	1 (6)
5	6 (33)	7 (39)	6 (33)	3 (17)	4 (22)	4 (22)	2 (11)

Note: 1 = less; 5 = more; M = mean; SE = standard error; SD = standard deviation.

Table 6 provides the same data for each of the variables related to personal decision, preparedness, and motivation to stay clean, as well as a rating of the environment in terms of being drug or alcohol free.

Table 6

Environment and Personal Decision, Preparedness, and Motivation Supporting Staying Clean/Being Sober (n = 18)

Statistic	Decision to stay clean	Prepared to stay clean	Present environment	Motivation
n valid	18	18	18	18
M	4.89	4.89	5.00	4.94
SE	.076	.111	.000	.056
SD	.323	.471	.000	.236
Frequency of rating, n (%)				
1	0	0	0	0
2	0	0	0	0
3	0	1 (5.6)	0	0
4	2 (11)	0	0	1 (5.6)
5	16 (89)	17 (94.4)	18 (100)	17 (94.4)

Note: 1 = less; 5 = more; M = mean; SE = standard error; SD = standard deviation.

From this descriptive data, the factors related to causes for drug use or relapse with the highest overall means included family problems and financial problems, followed by the desire to feel good and people/friends. These factors represent those perceived by participants to have the greatest effect as a cause for drug use and/or relapse. In addition, factors related to the strength of the individual's decision to stay sober, preparedness for the task, the cleanliness (drug-free nature) of present environment, and personal motivation to remain sober revealed similar responses across the factors demonstrating strength of decision, high motivation, and preparedness to remain clean/sober, as well as a current environment that is perceived to be highly drug/alcohol free.

Qualitative Data

The data are presented in terms of emergent themes related to the specific addiction triggers and recovery strategies as reported by participants in the study. Frequencies stemming from the individual participant responses were used to generate themes related specifically to the causes, patterns, and types of addiction and relapse triggers experienced by this population as well as types of responses, or strategies, which were felt to be most effective in terms of handling these triggers to avoid relapse for females in the Inland Empire community.

The data revealed four themes to form the open coding categories. These included reasons for first use, reasons for relapse, perceived personal risk factors, and personal plan for relapse prevention. Invariant constituents represent the variety of relevant key words and statements provided by respondents and related to a particular theme (Strauss, 1992). The number of invariant constituents identified for each of the open coding categories is noted in Table 7.

Table 7

Thematic Categories

Thematic category	No. of invariant constituents
Reasons for first use	10
Reasons for relapse	10
Personal risk factors	8
Personal plan for relapse prevention	7

Reasons for First-Time Use. The first open coding category revealed triggers that affect first-time users. The invariant constituents' central to this category included (a) peer pressure, (b) just to try it, (c) environment,

(d) amusement/partying, and (e) lack of parental guidance. Table 8 illustrates these invariant constituents and the associated frequencies.

Table 8

Reasons for First Use of Addictive Substance (n = 18)

Invariant constituent	n	(%)
Peer pressure	5	(28)
Just to try it	3	(17)
Environment	2	(11)
Amusement/partying/impulse	2	(11)
Lack of parental guidance	2	(11)
Family member	2	(11)
Liked it	1	(5.5)
To relax after work	1	(5.5)
Personal problems	1	(5.5)
Stay focused and get better grades	1	(5.5)

The most frequently cited reason for first using drugs or alcohol was thematized as peer pressure, or "for acceptance" (Participant 14). Participant 4 stated, "I think it was something all my friends were doing so I kinda fell in also." Similarly, Participant 18 cited, "Just to be cool and fit in." Participant 6 noted two of these elements, peer pressure as well as a lack of parental guidance, responding, "A combination of lack of parental guidance and influence of (former) friends led me to believe it was 'no big deal.'" Family or family members were mentioned by two participants, sometimes grouped with the influence of friends; for example, Participant 14 noted the influence of the "wrong crowd, even family."

In addition, three participants said they tried the drug or alcohol at first "just to do it because it was there" (Participant 17) or "just to try it" (Participant 7). Similarly, some noted doing it for amusement or partying. Participant 9 responded that she tried it "for amusement, a way to pass the time," while Participant 16 listed "teenage impulse, party and play." Other responses were mentioned by only a single participant, such as "I liked it" (Participant 1), or "to relax after work" (Participant 8), or "to remain focused on schoolwork" (Participant 12).

Reason for Relapse. The second open coding category, reasons for relapse, was determined by ten invariant constituents. The invariant constituents central to this category included (a) around the wrong crowd, (b) partner/significant other, and (c) financial problems. Table 9 illustrates these invariant constituents and the associated frequencies.

Table 9

Reasons for Ongoing Relapse (n = 18)

Invariant constituent	n	(%)
Around the wrong crowd	5	(28)
Partner/significant other	2	(11)
Financial problems	2	(11)
Relapsed with alcohol because she thought it was okay	1	(5.5)
Environment	1	(5.5)
Celebrating with a friend	1	(5.5)
False confidence	1	(5.5)
Personal problems	1	(5.5)
Desire to get high	1	(5.5)
To stay awake for late shift	1	(5.5)

The most frequent response in terms of specific reasons or perceived causes of relapse were related to social influences from friends, peers, or significant others. For example, Participant 4 noted the cause of using to be from being "around the wrong crowd." Participant 17 went into more detail, describing her relapse experience when responding to the question about reason for relapse and further shedding light on the reason for her motivation to stay clean: "Stupidity caused by peers. Only used once when I relapsed; promised myself I wouldn't be the one to introduce my kids to drugs. Clean ever since" (Participant 17). Two participants noted their "partner" or "significant other" as a trigger for relapse. Finally, Participant 6 declared that "environment, totally" was the perceived cause of her relapse. Within the concept of "environment," the participants frequently tended to describe social relationships, such as their "crowd," partner, family, friends, or peers.

Comparison of Reasons for Relapse with Reasons for First User. The survey responses in table 8 and table 9 were recoded in the categories listed in table 10 and compared by using a χ^2 table. This was done to determine the relationship between reasons for first-time use of an addictive substance and reasons for ongoing use and relapse, in order to investigate whether the relapse triggers were the same as the triggers of first-time use.

Table 10

Comparison of Reasons for Relapse with Reasons for First Use

	Observed n	Expected n	Residual
Personal stress	1	1.3	-.3
Social pressure	9	10.0	-1.0
Desire	7	3.8	3.2
Environmental, financial	3	5.0	-2.0
Total	20		

Note: The expected frequency is based on the original reasons for first use, and the observed frequency reflects the reasons for ongoing use or relapse.

Test Statistics	Reason for Relapse
χ^2	3.767
df	3
Asymp. sig. (2-sided)	.288

Relapse behavior appeared to be more often influenced simply by a desire or an urge to take the drug than would be expected based on the reasons for first use. Furthermore, environment and financial problems seemed to influence relapse behavior less often than would be expected based on the reasons for first use. However, χ^2 analysis of the data in table 10 shows that p is greater than .05. Therefore, the null hypothesis that there is no difference between the triggers for first use and the triggers for ongoing use or relapse cannot be rejected. Because the number of observations in some of the cells of table 10 was less than 5, the table was also analyzed with the Fisher exact test. For this test also, the resulting p value was greater than .05 ($p = .74$). Because of the small sample size, the test may not have had enough statistical power to detect a true difference if it does exist.

Perceived Risk Factors. Eight invariant constituents determined the third open-coding category, perceived risk factors. The invariant constituents central to this category included (a) environment, (b) old friends (social influences), and (c) financial problems. Table 11 illustrates these invariant constituents and the associated frequencies.

Table 11

Perceived Risk Factors (n = 18)

Invariant constituent	n	(%)
Environment	7	(39)
Old friends	4	(22)
Financial problems	2	(11)
Stress	1	(5.5)
Emotional problems	1	(5.5)
Former spouse threats	1	(5.5)
Everything	1	(5.5)
Nothing	1	(5.5)

In the last category, the perceived risk factors were explored, revealing that participants perceived "environment" (Participant 1) or more specifically, "bad environment" (Participant 4) to be a significant risk factor. Again, the results showed a common theme of friends or other people in that environment who were perceived as the significant factor within the environment affecting relapse and use behavior. For example, Participant 11 noted the risk factor of "being around people who drink, people offering me drinks," and "most likely being at a party or kickback." Similarly, Participant 18 noted, "people [she] hung with"; Participant 19 responded with "old friends, ways, and environment"; Participant 20 noted, "being around people that use"; and Participant 21 said, "hanging with people who use drugs."

Having "financial problems" (Participant 14) was also noted by two participants as a cause, or perceived risk factor for use and relapse. Another element noted by single participants included stress and emotional problems. For example, Participant 3 responded, "Emotional issues! But I truly find that church and prayer work for me at this time," providing insight into her mechanism for avoiding relapse by dealing with this risk factor.

Plans to Avoid Relapse. Seven invariant constituents determined the fourth open coding category, plans to avoid/fight relapse. The invariant constituents central to this category include (a) maintaining a good (clean) environment, (b) family, (c) keeping busy/focused, (d) attending meetings, (e) spirituality, and (f) "just say no," and (g) talk with someone I trust. Table 12 illustrates these invariant constituents and the associated frequencies.

Table 12

Plans to Avoid/Fight Relapse (n = 18)

Invariant constituent	n	(%)
Good environment	9	(50)
Family	4	(22)
Keep busy/focused	3	(17)
Meetings	3	(17)
Spirituality	2	(11)
Just say no	2	(11)
Talk with someone I trust	1	(5.5)

Participants in the study provided examples of how they planned or acted out strategies for reducing the risk and avoiding relapse. Just as negative associations were made with social influences in terms of drug/alcohol use and relapse, participants seemed to focus on personal support from positive social relationships for conquering the addiction and maintaining sobriety. For example, Participant 7 noted both the negative impact of social relationships with others who are using and the positive influence of sober friends, saying, "I don't plan on talking with people that I know are using, talk with the sober friends that I have made." Similarly, Participant 21 responded, "Hang with clean, sober, positive people." Participant 1 cited "family, spirituality, sobriety maintenance" as her mechanism for successful maintenance. Participant 3 specifically noted the support she had received at the rehabilitation home: "I plan to talk more and use my support here from Veronica's Home—it's the best support I have to keep my sobriety."

Participants also noted the perceived importance of staying focused, busy, and motivated to succeed on their own, both financially and personally. Participant 19, for example, stated, "[I] stay focused on the children and want to get my own money, care, etc.," and Participant 20 responded similarly with, "Stay focused and stay away from people that use." Finally, Participant 17 noted work, use of a social support person; "[I] handle my business or talk to someone that I trust about what is going on with me" (Participant 17).

ANSWERS TO RESEARCH QUESTIONS

The themes revealed from the analysis of the qualitative, open-ended survey question data along with the quantitative descriptive data can be used to address the research questions posed by the study. The quantitative and qualitative results reported represent the experiences and perceptions of the group as a whole. The themes and conclusions are presented according to each related research question.

Research Question 1: Experience of Relapse Triggers

The results of this mixed-method study provide insight into the perceived personal risks for relapse, relating to the perceived triggers or stressors in the participants' lives. As such, participants frequently noted the environment (7 of 18 participants, 39%), old friends (4 of 18 participants, 22%), and financial problems (2 of 18 participants, 11%) are major relapse risks or stressors in their lives. These findings were further supported qualitatively by reasons for relapse specifically cited by participants, which included being around the wrong crowd, partner, or significant other (a total of 7 of 18 participants, 39%), and financial problems (2 of 18 participants, 11%). The quantitative results also served to support these qualitative results, identifying the factors of family problems (mean of 3.19) and financial problems (mean of 3.29), followed by the desire to feel good (mean of 3.00) and people/friends (mean of 2.89) as having the greatest effect as a cause for drug use and/or relapse. Interestingly, triggers associated with events and holidays had means that were slightly lower (2.56 and 2.76 respectively).

Research Question 2: Causes, Patterns, and Categories of Relapse Triggers

Participants described their personal "reasons" for using drugs or alcohol the very first time and relapsing and the elements they felt affected the decision to use or reuse. Based on the results provided for research question one, it is evident that the sample as a whole tended to most often cite social influences of the "wrong crowd," family, partners/significant others, and friends as both causes of and risk factors for relapse/use. It is consistent with the study of Chong and Lopez, (2008) that states conflicts with other people and being in the company of alcohol or drug users were highly predictive of relapse.

The social influences of others, whether they be friends, family, or significant other, are indeed a significant part of anyone's environment, and as such, the identification of these elements serve to support the strength of overall environmental triggers and perhaps more clearly define this factor of "environment." In addition, financial concerns and problems was a factor mentioned throughout the analysis and related to different aspects of the research, being mentioned as a reason for relapse, as well as the perception of a risk factor.

Research Question 3: Are Relapse Triggers the Same as the Triggers of an Individual's Initial Drug Use?

Table 8 and table 9 show that many different factors and situations can trigger drug use among women. When the reasons for first-time use of an addictive substance (table 8) and the reasons for ongoing use or relapse (table 9) were categorized (as personal stress, social pressure, desire, or environmental/financial factors), comparison of the category distributions table showed that ongoing use and relapse behavior may have been more influenced by an actual desire for the substance and less influenced by environmental and financial factors. However, the differences were not significant. Thus, no firm conclusions can be drawn.

Research Question 4: Effective Responses

Participants provided open-ended answers to their perceived plan of action to avoid/fight relapse. The answers represent the thoughts of participants with regard to the perceived most effective response (or action) to the identified causes and triggers for drug/alcohol use. The responses were varied, but included strategies of maintaining a good (clean) environment, family support, keeping busy and/or focused, attending support meetings, personal spirituality, and applying a "just say no" attitude. Key to these elements is the common thread of external support, whether obtained through family, support meetings, or spirituality. Also critical, as perceived by participants, is reducing as much as possible, exposure to or experience with environmental stressor/triggers by remaining within a "clean" environment and remaining focused.

These results were further supported by the quantitative data, which demonstrated participants with highly rated strength of decision, high motivation, and sense of preparedness to remain clean/sober as well as a current environment that is perceived to be highly drug/alcohol free. These elements serve to support the participants' success at remaining drug/alcohol free and avoiding relapse.

SUMMARY OF RESULTS

Mixed methods analysis of interview data obtained from a sample of eighteen women housed in a treatment facility was completed with the assistance of SPSS statistical software and Microsoft Excel software. Results of the analysis were given, revealing four major themes generated from high frequency common responses, which were used to answer the first research question of the study. The themes identified (a) reason for first use, (b) reasons for relapse, (c) perceived individual risk factors, and (d) plans for remaining sober and fighting relapse.

Within these themes, participants revealed the perceived importance of peer pressure, environment, and impulsivity and amusement, in addition to a lack of parental guidance, as critical factors related to first-time and subsequent drug use. Social and financial causes for relapse were conveyed by participants, such as hanging around the wrong people, partner or significant other who uses, and financial problems. Risk factors were noted, which could be perceived triggers in general at this point. The results were supported by the quantitative findings indicating the most highly rated cause for drug use/relapse as family and financial problems, followed by the desire to feel good and the effect or influence of people or friends. The next chapter will provide a discussion of these results as they related to the research questions and the previous literature on the topic.

[CHAPTER FIVE]

Summary, Conclusions, and Recommendations

SUMMARY OF THE STUDY

The specific problem addressed by this study was to determine the nature, scope, and causes of pretreatment addiction triggers experienced by women with addiction disorders who live in the Inland Empire region of Southern California.

Pre-treatment relapsed triggers are a major barrier to relapse prevention among addicted individuals living in the community in the Inland Empire region. Therapists planning relapse intervention without adequate information on pretreatment triggers in the community will have difficulty planning relapse intervention goals. Therapists can improve relapse treatment intervention and prevention techniques if clinical information specifically describing drug and alcohol pretreatment triggers experienced by their clients is available.

Purpose: the study was developed to assess pretreatment triggers experienced by women with addiction problems who live in one area of Inland Empire.

A mixed qualitative and quantitative research method was used by the researcher in the study to qualitatively analyzed and explore the pre-treatment relapsed triggers lived experiences of participants and to quantitatively describe the perceived scale of influence of certain triggers and other related factors on individual experiences of addiction and/or relapse (Creswell, 2007, 2009).

According to the literature, qualitative research is the exploration of multiple meanings, socially and historically constructed, of individual experiences in order to develop a theory or pattern (Creswell, 2007, 2009). Qualitative studies focus on the importance of the participant's perspective and how it informs the personal meaning held by the participant (Creswell, 2007, 2009). Qualitative method also provides flexibility in exploring a subject, while allowing an in-depth investigation, potentially leading to the development of a new observation and the opportunity for further exploration of a study's prevalence, predictors, and sequence in other studies (Yoshikawa, et al., 2008). Qualitative methods are inquiry-based, enabling the exploration of an occurrence through questions, narrative descriptions, and analysis of emerging themes (Creswell, 2005). Qualitative methods provide a representation of the specific focus of the proposed study, based on the interpretation of lived experiences of the participants (Creswell, 2005; Neuman, 2003).

Patton (2002) explained why a qualitative approach may be useful for analyzing pretreatment trigger experiences. The issue is not whether objective research data are more desirable, valid, or meaningful than self-reported data, but rather that therapists cannot observe what individuals have done in their pretreatment addiction phase and lifestyle before coming for help or treatment.

Qualitative research has a focus on the detail and depth of information received from a relatively small population, which provides a rich and detailed understanding; whereas quantitative research provides the ability to form broad generalizations for a specific population (Patton, 2002). Quantitative method is appropriate for the study because analysis will be conducted on the perceived level of significance of various triggers and the strength of conviction and motivation of individuals to remain sober as identified via Likert scale survey questions. Quantitative research will provide the researcher with the ability to assess and compare numerical data, such as scaled data (Cozby, 2007).

Mixed methods research relies on both quantitative and qualitative methods that are consequences-oriented, problem-centered, and pluralistic (Creswell, 2009). According to Morrow (2007), qualitative research is appropriate when one needs to present a detailed and in-depth view of a phenomenon. Whereas quantitative methods can enable the researcher to get a broad understanding of a phenomenon, qualitative approaches are able to delve into complex processes and illustrate the multifaceted nature of a human phenomenon.

This study was designed to obtain a detailed understanding of the experiences of women with a history of addiction and vulnerability to relapse, as well as to generalize aspects of the data with regard to the perceived influence of certain elements that may serve as potential relapse triggers. Therefore, a mixed qualitative and quantitative method was used. In deciding the best research design for the study, the researcher asked the following questions: Which research design is best for this study? Which strategy will provide the most useful information for understanding relapse triggers? According to Patton (2002), if individuals or groups are the primary unit of analysis, then case studies of people or groups may be the focus for case studies. As a means of presenting the qualitative therapeutic approach, a descriptive case study design will be used. The case study design is a common method to develop a theory, evaluate programs, and develop interventions to existing programs and theories, allowing researchers to reveal and understand a multifaceted phenomenon (Baxter and Jack, 2008). Case study theory is based on a constructivist paradigm (Stake, 1995).

A case study research approach is useful for studies that have unknown variables, use interviews and observation, and have flexible guidelines (Creswell, 2005). Because the study was exploratory in nature, it lends itself to the use of case study methods in order to examine the potential for identification and understanding of triggers and planning of intervention to treat pretreatment addiction triggers to prevent relapse. Researchers use case studies when they are concerned with gathering real-life data from participants and creating an understanding of a specific phenomenon (Yin, 1994). Therefore, the current study will utilize the four stages of case study design as proposed by Yin (identification of required skills and review of protocol, application of the recommended procedures, implementation of the case study, and analyzing the evidence gathered) to explore and report on the experiences and perceptions of participants in terms of addiction triggers within the Inland Empire region.

An advantage of case study research is the close collaboration between the researcher and the participants (Baxter and Jack, 2008). Through this collaboration, the participants describe views of reality, providing a better understanding of the phenomenon and participant actions (Lather, 1992). In addition, the case study is frequently used because the researcher can use both quantitative and qualitative methods to examine the data (Yin, 2009). Case study theory enables researchers to answer questions such as "why" or "how" while still being able to incorporate the influence of a phenomenon (Baxter and Jack, 2008).

According to Stake (1995), a case study design "will ensure the topic of interest is well explored and that the essence of the phenomenon is revealed" (p.10). Case studies explore situations in which the topic being evaluated has no clear, single set of outcomes (Yin, 2009). A case study design is appropriate because the goal of the proposed study is to answer these "how" and "why" questions without manipulating the behavior of participants (Yin, 2009).

Both qualitative and quantitative data were obtained from the survey instrument. The data obtained from the open-ended questions were collected and analyzed using the four stages of case study design (Yin, 2009). The four stages presented by Yin (2009) include (a) the identification of required skills and review of protocol, (b) the application of the recommended procedures, (c) the implementation of the case study, and (d) the analysis of the evidence. The quantitative data from the survey will be analyzed using descriptive statistics. Within a descriptive study, the primary goal of the quantitative analysis is to "characterize a population or process based on certain attributes in that population or process" (Ott and Longnecker, 2010, p. 19). Therefore, quantitative descriptive statistics was used to examine the Likert scale items on the survey.

Incorporation of both qualitative and quantitative methods will allow for a broader and more complete picture of the experiences and perceived relative importance of various elements to the individual addiction and relapse experience(s).

The researcher plans used the following steps to initiate and complete the research:

First, the researcher employed a purposeful sampling plan. Purposeful sampling is a nonprobabilistic sampling method in which the researcher selects particular research locations and participants to increase probability and to provide the information necessary to answer the research questions of the study (Creswell, 2005). Selecting qualitative samples focuses on a collection of participants who will provide specific narratives to clarify and deepen the exploration of the study (Neuman, 2003). Quantitative research typically calls for larger sample sizes (over 30) (Ott and Longnecker, 2010), whereas qualitative research normally involves small sample sizes of participants, in contrast to quantitative research, which typically involves larger sample sizes (Creswell, 2005).

The population from which the sample was drawn consisted of women with a history of drug or alcohol problems who were residing in a shelter/treatment facility located in downtown San Bernardino city at the time of study recruitment. Although Creswell (2005) recommended that the size of a qualitative sample should range from 1 to 25 participants, and Polkinghorne (2005) recommended 5 to 25 participants, Patton (2002) stated that there are no specific rules for sample size, and stated, "Sample size depends on what you want to know, the purpose of the inquiry, what's at stake, what will be useful, what will have credibility, and what can be done with available time and resources" (p. 244). Therefore, the sample consisted of 20 to 25women. This sample size was based on number of females in the facility at any given time for treatment, the overall need to provide an in-depth analysis, and the expected availability of participants. Participation was voluntary.

Second, the survey instrument (appendix A) for this study included a set of Likert scale items for ratings as well as a set of open-ended questions for description of trigger experience(s). The questions appeared in the questionnaire designed for the study. Staff in the treatment center assisted with the distribution of the questionnaire and responded to any crisis related to the study. There were no incidents or crises. The researcher used the information gained from the data obtained from the questionnaire to develop a descriptive understanding of the problem of pretreatment triggers among this population (Moustakas, 1994). The data did not include or contain personal identifying information (names, addresses, employers, relatives, date of birth, telephone numbers, e-mail addresses, etc.). In a descriptive case study framework, the essence of the responses of the participants was extracted from the questionnaire and analyzed to provide information on the nature, characteristics, and experience of addiction triggers. In addition, a theory was generated to demonstrate the nature of pretreatment addiction triggers specific to this population, with the goal to allow development of better treatment options and strategies for dealing with relapse triggers among this population. Case study researchers are concerned with both individual responses as well as the interaction between responses (Yin, 1994). There are four stages that must be executed in order to develop a valid and reliable case study (Yin, 1994). The study was developed according to the four stages as presented by Yin (1994).

The first three stages in designing the case study protocol include (a) the identification of the skills required and to review the protocol; (b) the application of the recommended procedures, including identifying the type of research questions, establishing the degree of control the researcher exerts upon the study parameters, and the scope of focus of the study; and (c) conducting the case study through data collection and conducting interviews/group discussions .The fourth stage in designing a case study is analyzing the evidence that was gathered (Yin, 1994). This stage consists of examining, categorizing, tabulating, and combining the data to develop patterns and themes. Once the data have been analyzed, it is possible to present explanations for the results as well as implications for another research and ways in which the findings apply to other larger areas of interest or society as a whole (Yin, 1994).

The field study in this research focused on the problem of pretreatment addiction triggers as a real and ongoing problem among addicts returning to their community or receiving treatment in a community. Individuals with addiction disorders that have impacted or affected their lives in the community before treatment may continue to have the compulsion to obtain and re-experience the effect of drugs once they are treated and discharged into the community. These individuals have a significant risk of relapse, and it is essential for any relapse prevention method to respond to the individual triggers and stressors in their community (Kelly, et al., 2007). The current study sought to explore the nature and scope of pretreatment triggers experienced by addict female population in the Inland Empire region of Southern California with the purpose of assessing pretreatment addiction trigger experiences among this population.

As such, this mixed methods case study was designed to examine the perspectives of female participants struggling to defeat addiction to drugs or alcohol in the Inland Empire region and the specific causes and triggers that these women experience in their recovery process. Data were gathered through a survey instrument inclusive of both Likert scale and open-ended questions. The data were then analyzed through a case study analysis incorporating content analysis techniques. From the results of the study, the research sought to form a theory with regard to the common addiction triggers experienced by these participants.

CONCLUSIONS

A review of the results of the data analyses of the survey data incorporating both quantitative Likert scale questions as well as qualitative open-ended questions is provided. These results are used in an effort to answer the research questions of the study. The findings are therefore presented and discussed according to the associated research questions as well as related to the current literature.

Research Question 1: Experience of Relapse Triggers

The results of this mixed method study provides unique insight into the experiences and perceptions of participants to reveal personal risks for relapse, relating to triggers or stressors in the participants' lives. Prior research has defined common triggers as social influences of people a participant has previously used drugs with, money, drinking, social situations, and emotional/psychological factors such as anxiety, depression, and joy (Carroll, 1998). Qualitative results obtained from the open-ended survey questions revealed similar perceived risks for relapse in terms of the environment (39%), as well as with old friends (22%), and to a much lesser degree, from the stress of financial problems (11%). Further, reasons for relapse were offered by participants and included themes related to the company they keep (i.e., being around the wrong crowd, partner, or significant other, 39%), and financial problems (11%), both aligning with the prior research by Carroll.

The quantitative results also supported these findings, identifying the factors of family problems (mean of 3.19) and financial problems (mean of 3.29) as the highest ranked effect causing drug use and/or relapse. The findings suggesting the importance of family problems to relapse contrast previous research by Costello, et al., (2006), who found no significant increase in the risk of use among adolescents related to family problems.

In addition, participants noted the desire to feel good (mean of 3.00) and people/friends (mean of 2.89) as having an effect as a cause for drug use and/or relapse. In contrast to prior research by Rosenbloom (2009), who found relapse heightened during stress of holidays, results from this study failed to demonstrate the perceptions of strong triggers associated with events and holidays, which had mean averages that were lower (2.56 and 2.76 respectively).

Research Question 2: Causes, Patterns, and Categories of Triggers

The use of qualitative analysis tool and steps was very useful in identifying patterns, categories and levels of risk found in the data. This was significant because, the results provided for research question one, showed evidence that the sample as a whole tended to most often cite social influences of the "wrong crowd," family, partners/significant others, and friends as both causes and risks for relapse/use. These findings generally aligned with Carroll (1998).

The importance of social influences of others (i.e., friends, family, or a significant other) were shown to be an important piece of the environment in which we live and in which these recovering female addicts had to return to while successfully avoiding relapse. As such, the identification of these elements serves to help define the perception of environment for the participants, and how this environment serves to support their success or support their failure with subsequent relapse. In addition, financial concerns and problems was a factor mentioned in the analysis, although less strongly, which also aligned with findings of Carroll (1998).

Research Question 3: Are Relapse Triggers the Same as the Triggers for First Use?

The comparison of the reasons that trigger relapse with the original reasons that triggered first use sheds light on the fact that addicts do not have the same reasons for using drugs all the time. The original reason for first-time use of drugs may not be the same reason for ongoing use and relapse. People may use for the first time because they wanted to get high. Although they may then realize that drug use not only gives them a desirable high but also has other related problems, they continue to use despite the negative consequences experienced.

Research Question 4: Effective Responses

Participants shed light on their perceptions of their personal ways with which they planned to avoid relapse and as such, provided their thoughts with regard to the most effective treatment response (or action) to the personal causes and triggers for drug/alcohol use.

The variety of responses provided strategies of maintaining a good (clean) environment, family support, keeping busy and/or focused, attending support meetings, personal spirituality, and applying a "just say no" attitude. Key to these elements is the common thread of external support, whether obtained through family, support meetings, or spirituality. This finding aligns with that of Smith (2006) in which psychosocial interventions were used to maintain a focus on both abstinence and personal and social coping mechanisms. The coping mechanisms from this study also directly address Bradizza and Stasiewicz's (2003) taxonomy of relapse episodes, which states intrapersonal and interpersonal elements serve to support relapse.

Also critical, as perceived by participants, is reducing as much as possible, exposure to or experience with environmental stressor/ triggers by remaining within a "clean" environment and remaining focused. By reducing exposure, these participants were reducing the social pressures to relapse (part of the Bradizza and Stasiewicz, 2003, taxonomy). These qualitative results were further supported by the quantitative data, which demonstrated participants with highly rated strength of decision, high motivation, and sense of preparedness to remain clean/sober as well as a current environment that is perceived to be highly drug/alcohol free.

IMPLICATIONS AND TREATMENT

The results of the study highlight the critical nature of interpersonal relationships as part of the environment surrounding a recovering addict. In attempting to treat addiction triggers among the female population in the Inland Empire region, therapists, program managers, and other stakeholders must consider the social environment to which the recovering addict must return. Women are motivated by social relationships. This strength in one hand is a weakness in the other hand. Because, a lot of the triggers associated with drug and alcohol use among the female participants in this study may be related to social issues and challenges'. Besides chemical benefit expected, instinct and other motivation women relapsed behavior is well documented in this study is associated with relationship and social context.

That said, evidence from this study points to both the supportive nature of interpersonal relationships with "clean" family and friends, group support meetings, and others, while also noting the detrimental effects such relationships (when in a use/abuse environment) can have in terms of serving as a trigger for relapse and continued use of drugs/alcohol. Even the noted trigger effects of external elements such as financial problems may, in turn, be at least partially controlled by maintaining a positive, supportive, and clean (drug free) environment. This was evident in the reports of study participants, who demonstrated high ratings of perceived strength of decision to remain sober, high motivation to remain sober, and a sense of preparedness to remain clean/sober while they remained in an environment that was perceived to be highly drug/alcohol free and supportive, contributing to these positive self-perceptions of their own ability to remain clean and sober.

Remaining in an environment in which the recovering addict is able to reduce exposure to or experience with environmental stressor/triggers, including interpersonal triggers, the study participants were reducing the social pressures to relapse, as noted by Bradizza and Stasiewicz (2003). In addition, the environment provided a supportive base, which promoted positive and strong feelings in terms of their ability to remain sober.

Participants also called upon intrapersonal resources such as spirituality and focusing on their goals. Therapists and others responsible for the treatment of these individuals need to remain conscious of these influences, ensuring that the individual has proper support mechanisms in place, such as a support group, clean family life, and other positive social supports. At the same time, the individual must continue to avoid environments that may include friends and family who continue to use.

While the perceived reasons for relapse among these participants tended to align with the taxonomy of relapse episodes presented by Bradizza and Stasiewicz (2003), representative of both intrapersonal and interpersonal explanations, it was interesting to note that the findings on the opposite end of the spectrum (i.e., for avoidance of relapse) was a near mirror reflection of this taxonomy, suggesting that not only can the categories of the taxonomy elicit relapse, but that the antagonists to the categories of taxonomy can provide support for the avoidance of relapse.

This is a critical insight into the dichotomous nature of the relapse event suggested by these findings; interpersonal and intrapersonal triggers may put an individual at risk for relapse, but opposing interpersonal and intrapersonal support mechanisms may promote strength in the avoidance and successful defeat of such triggers in the individual's everyday environment.

Strategies such as motivational interviewing (Miller and Rollnick, 2009), in which the therapist focuses on the individual personal motivations for change, incorporating those motivations into the behavioral change plan, could be adapted to also include a focus on the individual interpersonal stressors and supports, allowing the individual to understand and maintain a consciousness with regard to the negative and positive influences of specific people and places in their lives and how these influences can seriously affect their personal ability to remain sober.

The evidence for the positive influence of interpersonal relationships also supports the concept of peer motivation (Tevyaw, et al., 2007) as an additional mechanism for avoiding and conquering relapse triggers and risk. These conclusions also align with suggestions of Smith (2006), who described the importance of interpersonal reflection as well as cognitive and action-based coping skills when seeking to avoid relapse. Bringing relapse prevention to a cognitive, conscious level within the individual recovering addict may be the key to their ability to remain in supportive versus high-risk environments, and their ability to avoid and fight relapse triggers.

Treatment

The key issue now is how we clinicians can have access to this information to plan relapse prevention. Addiction has a major influence on the way people, think, feel, behave, and live. It affects the whole person and has no regard for professional and nonprofessional, famous, star, and rich. Looking from the outside, individuals, families, friends, may think sometimes those affected is a sign of weakness, a disgrace to their family, unprofessional, or engaged in an illegal and criminal behavior they can stop if the heat is turn on them. The perception goes on and on.

None of the perception helps describe the problem or a better way of responding to the individual with the disease. In some ways, the help people offer tends to isolate the person or shame the person if they failed to respond to the help or treatment or did not recover. But addiction is not only a behavior problem or moral weakness it is a disease.

The researcher theorized drug use behavior of women is not driving by behavior of simply using drugs and personality problems. Drug use among women occurred in a relationship context and is influenced by peer and group or friends. Relationship context constitutes the natural makeup and disposition of women. Women were created to respond to the solitary, lonely, and lonesome problems of the sexes as helper, complementing and working alongside a person. Women's drug use behavior is driven not because of the drug needs but by relationship. Women use because they are in a relationship or unit of relationship peer or group or person or friends that use. The same is true of girls who got pregnant before their college years or during their college years. They got pregnant not because they wanted to have sex or be pregnant, but because they were in a complementing relationship that made them pregnant. This is why general psychological trends for understanding human behavior in the past focused on a person's behavior driven by physical needs or instinct may not always explain addiction behavior among women.

The study shows that women may not be driven by physical or instinct a lone but by peer or group relationship. Women do not always initiate a behavior because it satisfies their physical needs, but because they are in a relationship or unit of relationship with a peer or group or friends that do such things or require it. Women are driven by relationship more so than by physical needs, drive or personality problems. The analysis support this position because evidence from the analysis shows the main contributing factor for first-time women drug users is peers and for ongoing users is a group. Both unit peer and group are consistent with the makeup of women, who are created to respond to the void caused by loneliness, lonesomeness, and solitary lifestyle. Whether it is a nature or nurture issue is not the subject of this study.

This analysis outcome takes us in a new direction for planning treatment pertaining to women and addiction diagnosis. How we prepare to use this information in treatment planning, goals setting and objectives remain to be seen. It is easy to propose a simple rule that all drug and alcohol group treatment planning should be based or rooted in analysis showing identified triggers, categories, patterns and risk level found within a specific group. But this is not how present treatments are designed. However, it is a good news that we now have a qualitative model for group therapy and analysis steps already developed and ready for use if we ever decided to use it. We may have to train how to use qualitative therapy to facilitate group process and analysis which is not the objective of this study.

Meanwhile, we know women are different and so are the reasons for the first time they use and keep using drugs or alcohol. This information is critical for planning treatment for women. The first time a woman uses drugs may be because of (a) peer pressure, (b) just wanting to try or experiment, or (c) environment, lack of parental supervision, and family problems. Knowing this does not go far enough.

We now know that women's ongoing use of drugs and alcohol is related to being around the wrong crowd, relationship problems, and financial problems. What is insightful and revealing is that among female addicts, peer pressure appeared at the top among first-time factors for drug and alcohol use, and the wrong crowd was the factor for ongoing drug and alcohol use. This fact offers insight into the relationship context factor that influences drug and alcohol usage in female addicts. The context factor provides a clue for future drug treatment and intervention. The context factor of peer or group unit seems consistent with the natural nature of women who are created and formed to solve a problem specific to the "be alone" condition of the male. Women fulfill a role as they interact within a peer group or crowd, and they tend to be influenced by that peer or crowd rather than simply going off on physical needs alone.

Therefore, understanding a female addict's peers and group interaction is paramount for planning relapse interaction. To design a treatment plan without bringing the social context of interaction or working with the context of interaction peer or group may not be very effective. The therapist needs to find out what context the person is interacting in and who is in the peer or group context creating or influencing the relapse behavior.

A woman's peer or group context may be the people she gets along with. The peer or group context may be the environment that is facilitating or supporting or influencing the relapse behavior. This is the "risk environment." The risk environment is consistent with the risk women identified as the number one factor why they feel and want to use drugs or drink alcohol. In the risk environment are old friends, colleagues, a partner, family members, and other friends. Each element in the environment contributes different risk and level of risk (high or low).

One major problem envisioned by the researcher is the fact that limited resources in terms of human resources and financial resources are committed to this wider context of peers, groups, friends, colleagues, and family that influence or contribute to widespread female drug-use behaviors, dependence, trafficking, and to the drugs and alcohol made available or financed at any one time to influence the behavior of female drug use, dependence, and disease of addiction and finally death. The addict tends to be blamed for everything that goes wrong or that should have and should not have taken place.

The twenty-first century offers a new challenge for drug and alcohol treatment intervention practice that will include therapists making contact with the addict, peers, group, environment, and the people in the addict's context and unit of interaction for assessing the risk of the unit or peer, group, and environment. This means all of the addict's relationships must be included in the treatment.

A therapist must bring all those in the addict's peer and group unit and environment on board to work with the therapist to help change the peer, group, environment, and interaction context that is infected. Present treatment tends to be focused on the addict's behavior, personality, problems, and family, but not all individuals within the addict's interaction context or unit that support or enhance the drug behavior and dependence. Without this new direction, a person may be clean and sober, but the people in his unit of complementary interaction are not clean or sober or committed to the addict's recovery or are aware, and they may still influence the addict to keep using and relapse.

Treatment or support for a female addict to stay clean and sober has to be drawn from the addict's peer, group, environment, and interaction context to prevent anyone within the context from sabotaging the treatment because they were left out while still interacting with the addict or because they remain in the addict's complementary world of interaction and relationship. This is in keeping with the new understanding from this study that women are not influenced only by desire and physical needs but by their very nature to be in a relationship to complement and respond to isolation. Women are influenced by peers, group, and friends rather than physical needs alone. In the past or present recovery, addicts were told to avoid people and places. This was the easy thing to do, but it was not as effective as expected.

The new direction of female drug and alcohol relapse prevention treatment should focus on what the female was created for in the first place, which is to interact and respond to the "alone" problem of the male. We know that females use drugs at the interaction level doing the things they were designed to do. If the elements in the interaction environment are contaminated, the female addict will continue to interact with the peer, group, or environment. A lot of what the female does—dress, eat, drink, etc.— is at interaction level with a peer, group, friends, colleagues, family, children, and husband. All of these should be the focus of therapy.

It will be interesting how therapy in the twenty-first century will work to make the female addict not only the focus of therapy but her context of interaction and all elements in the environment contributing to her use of street drugs, prescription drugs, and alcohol. Equally important is to help prevent premature death of the addict by making the addict's health the focus of treatment. Some people come to treatment already with undiagnosed organ problems.

Limitations

The study was limited to an exploration of the perceptions of a sample of women recovering from addiction disorders who lived in a single treatment home in the Inland Empire region. Therefore, the findings of the study represent the specific relapse and addiction trigger experiences by this particular group of women within each individual's personal community environment, as no one's life and community experiences are identical, from family experiences to large community experiences. The use of the questionnaire may have limited the results by not allowing for the participant to fully express her perceptions and experiences.

RECOMMENDATIONS FOR FUTURE RESEARCH

Because of the significant limitation of the present study regarding lack of opportunity for in-depth open discussion from individual participants about their specific personal experiences, a qualitative exploration, perhaps from a phenomenological perspective, using interviews or group process is recommended in order to obtain a more in-depth understanding. The results of this study suggest the importance of interpersonal experiences, particularly the influence of peers, both on the first use of an addictive substance and on relapse behavior. Research in the form of an interview process is needed to find ways to help addicted individuals identify specific interactions with others that influence addictive behavior, including positive aspects of interactions with supportive persons on the one hand and negative aspects of interactions with those who function as addiction triggers on the other hand. Helping to define positive versus negative relationships is important, because the line may not be clear in some circumstances. Further qualitative research should then focus on identifying techniques that addicted individuals can use to foster positive relationships, to avoid relationships that trigger addictive behavior, and to deal with addiction-triggering relationships that cannot be avoided. Because being in a "good environment" was named by half of the participants as an important part of their plans to avoid or fight relapse, additional research should also focus on ways to help individuals to find or create such an environment for themselves.

On the other end of the spectrum, further quantitative research using Liker scale items regarding the perceived triggers and supports that influence addicted individuals would be able to provide more generalizable information on the relative strength of these various influences. Such information gathered from a large sample would serve to inform practice. A more comprehensive questionnaire including more variables than the one used in the present study should be used to gain a better understanding of the most significant relapse triggers within a specific population. For example, participants of this study rated financial problems as an important cause of relapse (table 5). More specific information on such variables would enable more targeted treatment and options to promote the avoidance and success over triggers and risks for relapse.

SUMMARY

Therapists continue to struggle with developing successful interventions and strategies to assist the successful transition of addicts returning to the community from which they were once users, a community by default, replete with addiction relapse trigger challenges. As such, it is essential for relapse prevention treatment to respond to the varied individual triggers and stressors in each addict's community (Kelly, et al., 2007). This mixed methods case study was designed to explore the perspectives and experiences of a sample of female addicts from the Inland Empire region of Southern California who are struggling to defeat addiction to drugs or alcohol, in terms of specific causes and triggers that these women experience in their recovery process, their strength of conviction to remain sober, and how they plan to accomplish that goal.

Data were gathered through a survey instrument inclusive of both Likert-scaled and open-ended questions and were analyzed through a case study analysis incorporating content analysis techniques, providing the results of the study.

Study results suggested the critical nature of interpersonal relationships as part of the environment surrounding a recovering addict, with evidence pointing to the supportive nature of interpersonal relationships such as family, friends, and group supports, while also noting the detrimental effects of such relationships when these relationships represent a negative influence in terms of drug use and abuse, serving as a trigger for relapse and continued use of drugs/alcohol.

The researcher plans to use these results in three ways: (1) to plan strategies for relapse prevention based on the recovering addict's pretreatment triggers; (2) to make the information publicly available so that it can be used by all involved with the problem of addiction; and (3) to contribute to the training of therapists and others involved in solving the problems of addiction.

Planning Strategies

Therapy should focus on enabling a cognitive, conscious level within the individual recovering addict to decipher supportive interpersonal relationships and supportive, positive environments from those that may serve as relapse triggers. This level of cognition may be the key to their ability to remain in supportive versus high-risk environments and their ability to avoid and fight relapse triggers. This study has clearly described pretreatment addiction triggers associated with drug and alcohol use and relapse.

Contribute to Training

The current study provides general information about pretreatment triggers. Clinicians will need to conduct assessments on an individual basis to determine specific triggers and associated symptoms to help their clients plan behavior responses and develop coping skills. Future individual and group therapies for drug and alcohol addictions must be based on an understanding of the way each individual client experiences the pathway to relapse and addiction (trigger→symptoms associated with a specific trigger→craving→behavior→relapse and addiction). Future treatment should focus on helping individual clients to identify these steps in regard to their own behavior and on ways to build specific skills for responding to such situations in order to prevent relapse. Thus, the research plans to contribute to the training of therapists not only in regard to methods of generating information on pretreatment relapse triggers as input for analysis, but also regarding methods for developing specific individualized interventions based on the empirically generated data on pretreatment triggers.

Drug use has certain complexities and mechanisms that are always influenced by the environment, people, places, and things. Addicted individuals depend on drugs to experience an expected reward, however negative the ultimate consequences are. The reasons for drug use are not static—they do not remain the same throughout the addicted individual's life. Therefore, in planning interventions, therapists and counselors should help the client to continue to assess changes in reasons and triggers for drug use, as well as their own behavior in response to the triggers. Therapists must also take into account the illegality of drug use, as well as the ability of addicted individuals to manipulate others or influence those dependent on them and to put in place structures that give them access to drugs. Ultimately, assessment should focus not only on triggers but on health issues because of the possibility that their addicted clients living with undiagnosed organs badly damaged due to prolonged use and exposure to drugs or alcohol. Physical assessment is critical in drug and alcohol treatment. Do not start treatment without paying close attention to the physical health of individuals. The major issue now is how this information provided in this study will help inform drug and alcohol treatment planning for women not dictate it.

REFERENCES

Addolorato, G., L. Leggio, L. Abenavoli, and G. Gasbarrini. 2005. "Neurobiochemical and clinical aspects of craving in alcohol addiction: A review." *Addictive Behaviors* 30: 1209–1224.

American Psychiatric Association. 2004. *Diagnostic and Statistical Manual of Mental Disorders* (4th ed.). Washington, DC: Author.

Baxter, P., and S. Jack. 2008. "Qualitative case study methodology: Study, design, and implementation for novice researchers." *The Qualitative Report* 13(4): 544–559.

Bottlender, M., & Soyka, M. (2004). Impact of craving on alcohol relapse during, and 12 months following, outpatient treatment. *Alcohol & Alcoholism*, 39, 357-361.

Beck, A. 1993. *Cognitive Therapy and the Emotional Disorders.* New York, NY: Penguin.

Boggan, W. 2008. "Alcohol and you." Retrieved from http://www.chemcase.com/alcohol.

Bradizza, C. M., and P. R. Stasiewicz. 2003. "Qualitative analysis of high-risk drug and alcohol-use situations among severely mentally ill substance abusers." *Journal of Addictive Behavior*

28: 157–169. Retrieved from http://www.sciencedirect.com.

Chong, J. and Lopez, D. (2008) *Am Indian Native Ment. Health Res.* Retrieved from Http://www.

Califano, J. A. 2006. "Alcohol and teen drinking." *National Center on Addiction and Substance Abuse.* Retrieved from http://www.focusus.com/alcohol.html.

Carroll, K. M. 1998. Therapy manuals for drug addiction. *Manual 1: A cognitive behavior approach: Treating Cocaine Addiction.* US Department of Health and Human Services. Retrieved from http://archives.drugabuse.gov/pdf/CBT.pdf.

Center for Substance Abuse Treatment. 2005. *Substance abuse treatment for persons with co-occurring disorders.* Treatment Improvement Protocol (TIP) Series 42. DHHS Publication No. (SMA) 05-3992. Rockville, MD: Substance Abuse and Mental Health Services Administration.

_____2007. *Screening, assessment, and treatment planning for persons with co-occurring disorders.* COCE Overview Paper 2. DHHS Publication No. (SMA) 07-4164. Rockville, MD: Substance Abuse and Mental Health Services Administration, and Center for Mental Health Services. Retrieved from http://www.coce.samhsa.gov/cod_resources/PDF/OP2-ScreeningandAssessment-8-13-07.pdf.

Chenail, R. J., and P. Maione. 1997. "Sensemaking in clinical qualitative research." *The Qualitative Report* [online serial], 3(1). Retrieved from http://www.nova.edu/ssss/QR/QR3-1/sense.html.

Cherry, K. n.d. "What is the amygdala?" Retrieved from http://psychology.about.com/od/aindex/g/amygdala.html.

Connolly, K. M., S. F. Coffey, J. S. Baschnagel, D. J. Drobes, and

M. E. Saladin. 2009. "Evaluation of the Alcohol Craving Questionnaire-NOW factor structures: Application of a cue reactivity paradigm." *Drug Alcohol Dependency* 103(1-2): 84–91. doi: 10.1016/j.drugalcdep.2009.03.019.

Costello, E. J., M. Sung, C. Worthman, and A. Angold. 2006. "Pubertal maturation and the development of alcohol use and abuse." Retrieved from http://www.elsevier.com.

Cozby, P. C. 2007. *Methods in Behavioral Research* (7th ed.). Boston: McGraw Hill.

Creswell, J. W. 2005. *Educational Research: Planning,Conducting, andEevaluating Quantitative and Qualitative Research* (2nd ed.). Upper Saddle River, NJ: Pearson Education.

_____2007. *Educational Research: Planning ,Conducting, and Evaluating Quantitative and Qualitative Research.* Upper Saddle River, NJ: Pearson Education.

_____2009. *Research Design: Qualitative, Quantitative, and Mixed Methods Approaches.* Thousand Oaks, CA: Sage Publications, Inc.

Dean, D. A. 2009. "Drug addiction." Retrieved from http://www.csun.edu/~vcpsyooh/students/drugs.html.

"Drug addiction triggers." 2010. Retrieved from http://www tarzana.org.

Drug-Rehabs.org. 2009. "Drug rehab and alcohol addiction treatment information." Retrieved from http://www.drug-rehabs.org.

Enkel, T., R. Spanagel, B. Vollmayr, and M. Schneider. 2010. "Stress triggers anhedonia in rats bred for learned helplessness." *Behavioural Brain Research* 209(1): 183–186. doi: 10.1016/j.bbr.2010.01.042.

Gerwe, C. F. 2000. "Chronic addiction relapse treatment: A study of the effectiveness of the high-risk identification and prediction treatment model: Part I." *Journal of Substance Abuse Treatment* 19(4): 415–427.

Harris, M., R. D. Fallot, and R. W. Berley. 2005. "Special section on relapse prevention: Qualitative interviews on substance abuse relapse and prevention among female trauma survivors." *Psychiatric Services* 56: 1292–1296.

Hoepfl, M. C. 1997. "Choosing qualitative research: A primer for teaching education." Retrieved from http://scholar.lib. vt.edu/journal/jee/v.html.

Hunter, K., S. Hari, C. Egbu, and J. Kelly. 2005. "Grounded theory: Its diversification and application through two examples from research studies on knowledge and value management." *Electronic Journal of Business Research Methods* 3(1): 57–68.

Jaffe, A. 2010. "Trigger." Retrieved from http://www.psychologytoday. com/blog/all-about-addiction/201003/triggers-and-relapse-craving-connection-addicts.

Kalivas, P. W., and C. O'Brien. 2008. "Drug addiction as a pathology of staged neuroplasticity." *Neuropsychopharmacology* 33: 166–180. doi:10.1038/sj.npp.1301564.

Kelly, T. J., J. M. Gaither, and L. J. King. 2007. "Relapse." In J. E. Lessenger and G. F. Roper (eds.), *Drug Courts: A New Approach to Treatment and Rehabilitation.* New York, NY: Springer, 377–388.

Koob, G. F., and M. Le Moal. 2008. "Addiction and the brain antireward system." *Annual Review of Psychology* 59: 29–53. doi: 10.1146/annurev.psych.59.103006.093548.

Lather, P. 1992. "Critical frames in educational research: Feminist and post-structural perspectives." *Theory into Practice* 31(2): 87–99.

Le Doux, J. E. 2008. "Amygdala." In *Scholarpedia*. Retrieved from http://www.scholarpedia.org/article/Amygdala.

Madigan, L. 2010. "Strategies for fighting meth." Retrieved from http://www.illinoisattorneygeneral.gov/methnet/fightmeth/treatment.html.

Mathison, C., J. Alexander, and J. Rizzo. n.d. "Introduction to the brain" Retrieved from http://its.sdsu.edu/multimedia/mathison/limbic/index.html.

Merriam, S. 1998. *Qualitative Research and Case Study Applications in Education*. San Francisco: Jossey-Bass.

Miller, W. R., and S. Rollnick. 2009. "Ten things that motivational interviewing is not." *Behavioural and Cognitive Psychotherapy* 37: 129–140.

Morrow, S. L. 2007. "Qualitative research in counseling psychology: Conceptual foundations." *The Counseling Psychologist* 35(2): 209–235.

Moustakas, C. E. 1994. *Phenomenological Research Methods*. Thousand Oaks, CA: Sage Publications.

National Institute on Drug Abuse. 2009. *Principles of Drug Addiction Treatment: A Research-Based Guide* (2nd edition). NIH Publication No. 09–4180. Retrieved from http://www.nida.nih.gov/podat/podatindex.html.

_____2010. *Drugs, Brains, and Behavior: The Science of Addiction*. Retrieved from http://www.drugabuse.gov/publications/science-addiction.

Neill, J. 2009. "Analysis of professional literature: Class 6: Qualitative research I." Retrieved from http://www.wilderdom.com/OEcourses/PROFLIT/Class6Qualitative1.htm.

Neuman, W. L. 2003. *Social Research Methods: Qualitative and*

Quantitative Approaches (5th ed.). Boston, MA: Allyn & Bacon.

Ott, R. L., and M. Longnecker. 2010. *An Introduction to Statistical Methods and Data Analysis* (6th ed.). Belmont, CA: Brooks/ Cole, Cengage Learning.

Pate, L. 2009. "Triggers." Retrieved from http://www.kci.org/meth_ info/lori/triggers.htm.

Patton, M. Q. 2002. *Qualitative Research and Evaluation Methods.* Thousand Oaks, CA: Sage Publications.

Polkinghorne, D. E. 2005. "Language and meaning: Data collection in qualitative research." *Journal of Counseling Psychology* 52(2): 137–145.

Porrino, L. J., J. B. Daunais, H. R. Smith, and M. A. Nader. 2004. "The expanding effects of cocaine: Studies in a nonhuman primate model of cocaine self-administration." *Neuroscience and Biobehavior Review* 27: 813–820. doi:10.1016/j. neubiorev.2003.11.013.

Reusch, W. n.d. "Alcohols." *Virtual Text of Organic Chemistry.* Retrieved from http://www.cem.msu.edu/~reusch/VirtualText/ alcohol1.htm#alcnom.

Rosenbloom, D. L. 2009. "Holidays, triggers, and willpower." *Journal of Substance Abuse Treatment* 36: 7.

Smith, C. H. S. 2006. *Exploring chronic sorrow as a relapse trigger in female victims of child abuse currently seeking treatment for substance abuse.* Doctoral dissertation, University of Arkansas for Medical Sciences. Retrieved from ProQuest database.

Stake, R. E. 1995. *The Art of Case Study Research.* Thousand Oaks, CA: Sage.

Sterk-Elifson, C. 1995. *Determining Drug Use Patterns among Women: The Value of Qualitative Research Methods*. Bethesda, MD: US Department of Health and Human Services, National Institute on Drug Abuse. Retrieved from PsycETRA. EBSCOhost.

Stewart, J. 2008. "Psychological and neural mechanisms of relapse." *Philosophical Transactions of The Royal Society, Biological Sciences* 363: 3147–3158. doi: 10.1098/rstb.2008.0084.

Strauss A Corbin J (1998) *Basics of qualitative research techniques and procedures for developing grounded theory* Second edition Thousand Oaks: Sage Publications

Taylor, C. 2010. *Enough! A Buddist Approach to Finding Release from Addictive Patterns*. Ithaca, NY: Snow Lion Publications.

Tevyaw, T. O., B. Borsari, S. M. Colby, and P. M. Monti. 2007. "Peer enhancement of a brief motivation intervention with mandated college students." *Psychology of Addictive Behaviors* 21(1): 114–119. Retrieved from http://web.ebscohost.com/ehost/detail?Vid.

"Triggers." 2010. Retrieved from http://www.drug-rehabs.org/articles/114?

Urell, B. 2010. "Drug and alcohol addiction relapse triggers—A really simple guide to addiction relapse prevention." Retrieved from http://ezinearticles.com/?Drug-and-Alcohol-Addiction-Relapse-Triggers--A-Really-Simple-Guide-to-Addiction-Relapse-Prevention&id=2088664.

US Department of Health and Human Services (USHHS). 2009. Substance Abuse and Mental Health Services Administration Center for Substance Abuse Treatment. "Therapy Manual for Drug Addiction." Bethesda, MD: NIDA.

Vieten, C., J. A. Astin, R. Buscemi, and G. P. Galloway. 2010.

"Development of an acceptance-based coping intervention for alcohol dependence relapse prevention." *Substance Abuse* 31(2): 108–116.

Wechsler, H., G. Dowdall, G. Maenner, J. Gledhill-Hoyt, and H. Lee. 1998. "Changes in binge drinking and related problems among American college students between 1993–1997." *Journal of American College Health* 47(2): 57–68.

Yin, R. K. 1994. *Case Study Research, Design and Methods*. Thousand Oaks, CA: Sage Publications.

_____2009. *Case Study Research, Design and Methods* (4ᵗʰ ed.). Thousand Oaks, CA: Sage Publications.

Yoshikawa, H., T. S. Weisner, A. Kalil, and N. Way. 2008. "Mixing qualitative and quantitative research in developmental science: Uses and methodological choices." *Developmental Psychology* 44(2): 344–354. doi: 10.1037/0012-1649.44.2.344.

Young, R. S., J. R. Joe, J. Hassin, and D. St. Clair. 2001. "Addressing psychosocial issues and problems of co-morbidity for Native American clients with substance abuse problems: A conference proceedings." *American Indian and Alaska Native Mental Health Research* 10: 2. Retrieved from ProQuest Psychological Journals.

APPENDIX A
ASSESSMENT OF COMMUNITY ADDICTION TRIGGERS

This questionnaire can help the researcher assess your experience with addiction relapse triggers. How serious is it? What can be done to prevent relapse?

It is important to answer all questions giving your best answer. Information obtained in this survey is for research purposes only and is for use in this study only.

First and last initial_____ Gender (circle) M F_____Age____

Education: ___Some high school   Ethnicity:

           ___High school grad   _____African American

           ___Some college   _____Hispanic

           ___Associate's degree   _____Asian

           ___Bachelor's degree   _____Caucasian (White)

           ___Graduate/Masters +   _____Other: _____

Town _____ Any arrest for drug/alcohol use _____

Age first used _____

Last time clean _____ Drug of choice _____

Past drug treatment _____

Please respond to the following by giving your best rating Less (1)
More (5)

How would you rate the strength of your decision to stay clean and
sober?   1 2 3 4 5

How prepared do you feel to stay clean and sober?   1 2 3 4 5

How clean (drug/alcohol free) is your present environment? 1 2 3 4 5

How would you rate your motivation to stay clean and sober?

1 2 3 4 5

How would you rate the effect of family problems as cause for drug use?

1 2 3 4 5

How would you rate the effect of financial problems as cause for drug
use?   1 2 3 4 5

How would you rate the effect/influence of people or friends as cause
for relapse?   1 2 3 4 5

How would you rate the effects of certain events as cause for relapse?

1 2 3 4 5

How would you rate the effect of holidays as cause for drug use?

1 2 3 4 5

How would you rate the desire for feeling good as cause for drug use?

1 2 3 4 5

How would you rate the desire to feel high as cause for relapse?

1 2 3 4 5

Please describe briefly

1. What was the major reason you first used drugs or alcohol?

_____

_____

_____

2. Last time you relapsed, what were your reasons? What do you
    feel specifically affected that decision?

_____

_____

_____

3. What do you think puts you at more risk to use drugs or alcohol?

_____

_____

_____

4. What do you plan to do now to fight relapse?

_____

_____

_____

ABOUT THE AUTHOR

Dr. Richard Corker-Caulker has been in clinical practice for many years, working with individuals and groups battling drug and alcohol problem and challenges. In this book, he uses qualitative analysis methods to identify and describe drug and alcohol relapse triggers, categories, patterns, and risk levels among women.